THE ANSWER

A "Change Your Heart" Book

THE ANSWER

A "Change Your Heart" Book

Ann Marie Hassett

Springtime Publishing Company
Beaverton, Oregon

The Answer
A "Change Your Heart" Book
by Ann Marie Hassett

Published by:
Springtime Publishing Company
19928 SW Inglis Drive
Beaverton, OR 97007-6095. U.S.A.
springtime.publishing@comcast.net

Unattributed quotations are by Ann Marie Hassett

ISBN, print ed. 0-9748275-0-9

First Printing 2004

Printed in the United States of America

Publisher's Cataloging-in-Publication
(Provided by Quality Books, Inc.)

> Hassett, Ann Marie.
>   The answer : a "change your heart" book / Ann Marie
> Hassett.
>   p. cm.
>   Includes bibliographical references.
>   ISBN 0-9748275-0-9
>
>   1. Parenting. 2. Parenting—Religious aspects—
> Christianity.   I. Title.

HQ755.8.H37 2005   649'.1
                           QBI04-800120

To the Lord of Heaven and Earth

To the Spirit:
Who Guides

To the Son:
Who Makes All Ways New

Thank You!

Acknowledgements

First I want to give my heartfelt thanks to God, my creator, who helped me through these very difficult times and to the saints in Heaven who listened to my call and also asked God to help me. Thank you.

I want to thank my husband and my kids for being open and willing to try new things. I truly believe that this experience has strengthened our family and our relationships with each other.

Last, I want to thank Kate Wilson, a student at the University of Portland, my oldest daughter, and my husband for their help with some of the editing and organization of this book.

Table of Contents

Contents

Notes

L earn and believe that God's ways are true ways. Devour His words so that they become part of you. His ways of love shal become the only acceptable path. Understand what it means when you hear that Christ came so that we may have life; life not as the world gives but as God gives; a life with a continuous daily focus and purpose for you.

I t is important to remember that only God gives the answer as to what to do and how to live life well. We all can look to God for the answers to what looks like problems. Self-centered desires virtually disappear when we judge everything by checking internally whether a decision is driven by self-pleasure versus a centered desire for God's will. Refuse self-centered gratification and internally tell God, "You decide if it is a good idea." If it is God's will, events etc. easily fall into place. Large and small problems or needs will be answered if people turn to God asking the heartfelt question, "What shall I do, God?"

Preface

This book was written in order to tell the true story of how we asked God to come into our chaotic family and how He showed us a new way to live.

God, who cares deeply about his people, has given The Answer, which brought and continues to bring love, peace, and happiness. By believing, trusting and following God's directions, love spreads, life becomes easier, relationships improve, and joy will follow.

My hope is that the positive changes outlined in this book will spread too everyone, especially parents.

— Ann Marie Hassett
June 28, 2004

Bibliography

The New American Bible. Oxford University Press. 1990.

The New International Version Bible. [Online] Available. http://www.biblegateway.com, 28 June 2003.

The Message Bible. [Online] Available. http://www.biblegateway.com, 28 June 2003.

1

HEARTBROKEN

Life was hard. I had four children, and the baby was two months old. I wanted the house to be perfect — but the light colored linoleum and carpet were difficult to keep clean. There were so many toys. The laundry kept growing. We had just moved into a new house. The kids kept tracking in mud from our unfinished yard. Breakfast, lunch, and dinner seemed to meld into one continuous burden. I had so much work to do.

The two oldest children were difficult to manage. They wouldn't eat or take naps when I wanted them to. I was angry. My oldest child was destructive and hurt her siblings. Crying and fights were routine.

My husband was always working at his job, working in the garage, or working on the yard. No one called to talk. No one was there to help. I was always alone.

I was afraid to let the oldest child play outside, because she got hurt every time. Then, I found clumps of hair under the couches. I found hair under her bed. I looked at her head. She had scratched an open sore there. The hair was gone within a one-inch diameter.

I was scared! I didn't know what to do. I was heartbroken.

2

I WAS HAPPY AT FIRST

In the beginning of our marriage I was happy. When we started having children, I loved teaching our firstborn child and watching her learn. It was so very exciting. She was on my mind often. I treated her as if she were much older than her age because she was always over the 99th percentile for height and weight; she looked twice her age even at two. She learned very fast and consequently, we expected even more from her. When she made mistakes we would unjustly reprimand her instead of being logical, kind, and gentle. We forgot that she was just a small child. Since I was the main caregiver, I was most to blame for this injustice. I believed that children were basically naughty. They had to be taught to be good with punishment, irritation, or anger. I assumed that our child was trying to get away with things, never expecting that questioning, and trying new things, was how a child learns. Thus, I demanded that my first child be wise beyond her years.

When my second child was born, my oldest noticed a loss of attention. She acted out in ways that, as parents, we did not like. We often punished her for her actions and got angry, giving her negative attention for her actions.

With four people now in the family, my husband took up wood-working as a hobby to save money on furniture for our home. The hobby made him even busier, distancing him from both the family and the children, making his own children into burdens.

After five years and three kids, my husband and I were drained. Our family life was quickly losing its luster and was becoming no fun. The kids had so much energy and they weren't getting any easier to manage. The oldest was jealous of the second child, and neither of them were the perfect angels that we had expected. I continuously saw their faults and diligently tried to correct them by saying "no, no, no" to everything. I tried to be a firm and unbending parent. I gave threats of impending trouble. Finally I'd get angry because of my own lack of inaction. I'd be tough with the kids and louder. I'd show them I meant it. My husband thought I was too tough. He would give in to them. My oldest child would exploit this disparity between parenting styles. She would insist until she got her way, or she would have a tantrum. Times were hard, but I knew I was trying to be good.

Times were definitely difficult.

Years before this, before I ever got married, during my grade school and high school years, I wanted to be good. I wanted to love God. I wanted to obey the commandments. I wanted to go to heaven. I wanted it for others, too. There were some key moments where I prayed so hard for my family to be peaceful, for others to speak kindly, and for people to speak God's name reverently. I knew I was imperfect, too.

During college, I prayed and attended church daily with an old friend in mind. My prayers continued as I went into the work force. Soon I fell in love with God.

Eventually I dated the person who was to be my husband. We talked about God *all* the time and went to church together daily. I dreamed of having a perfectly God-filled family in our marriage.

And now...

Here I was, a mom, in all this trouble with the kids. I thought I could make my kids be good. They would believe and go to heaven. I was following all the Commandments as best I could and staying within the church's teachings. I felt a little smug about my life and then started worrying about how some people in the world would miss seeing God.

The days were hard. My kids were just stubborn and wild. Being a parent was tough, but I could keep going.

My concern turned from myself to the larger population in the world. I hoped they believed and followed God like I was trying to, but I was too busy to help anyone else. I thought, "How could I help others go to heaven?" An idea emerged. "Everyone in the world touches someone. There's the belief that all the circles between the people in the world are connected. God would help everyone if I just asked him to. I'd pray for everyone that I saw and ask God to help them. They would affect each other."

Things were tough for me, but I could do that. I'd pray while I was driving.

Life was hard but I could give up all my hardships as a gift to God. I would continue with the family, I would continue to pray for others.

Our fourth child was only a few months old. We had moved into a larger house with a huge unfinished yard. The work never ended. The children were fighting and breaking things.

The loving feelings within the family were quickly vanishing. I pondered the Biblical teaching that children are a blessing and I thought, "No, they are not." I felt guilty for disbelieving but I could not deny the feelings. Pondering more, needing God, and feeling guilty, I decided that God's words must be true. The blame could not lie with God, or with my children. The fault could only be in myself. I must have been doing something wrong. I didn't know what it could be.

Trusting God's words again, I believed, "His words have to be true." I prayed, "I'm sorry for not believing you under all this work God." From that day on our life started to change

Soon thereafter, a single thought came to me, **"Just do what you can do."** I felt that these words were a direction. When I came across some papers, I would pick them up and throw them away. I'd put away the dishes from the dishwasher when I had a moment. The days grew a little easier and I was less stressed about housework. The kids were still difficult and disobedient, but I relaxed. Completing every task instantly was not the priority. The work would be done as soon as the chance came.

Early one morning, while in the laundry room I heard a thought in my mind that said, **"See how God loves you. See the mountains.**

See the trees.″ I was awestruck at these words! Over the next few days I pondered their sweetness. The phrase comforted me and made me happy. The work remained and the kids were just as difficult.

God could remedy the problems, especially the difficulties my oldest daughter was having. I recollected the action needed when you desired something. The Bible spoke of prayer.

> The real widow, who is all alone, has set her hope on God and continues in supplications and prayers night and day. (1 Timothy 5:5)

> Again, [amen] I say to you, if two of you agree on earth about anything for which they are to pray, it shall be granted to them by my heavenly Father. For where two or three are gathered together in my name, there am I in the midst of them. (Matthew 18:19–20)

Another verse spoke of praying in Jesus' name:

> And whatever you ask in my name, I will do, so that the Father may be glorified in the Son. If you ask anything of me in my name, I will do it. If you love me, you will keep my commandments. And I will ask the Father, and he will give you another Advocate to be with you always, the Spirit of truth, which the world cannot accept, because it neither sees nor knows it. But you know it, because it remains with you, and will be in you. (John 14:13–17)

Two thousand years later, God would honor this promise to hear and answer me if I completely trusted and had faith in Him. I'd keep my mind on Him all day. The Bible spoke of praying together and also praying in Jesus' name; I knew my husband and I needed to pray together to make things better at home. Only God could fix our problems. I explained to him all the problems I was having with the kids. My husband was not aware of the problems, thus he disagreed with me. He felt reluctant and uncomfortable praying, especially out loud. I persisted, explaining the problems and the verses in the Bible. It meant so much to me. Our oldest needed help so much that I persisted until my husband accepted my request. We needed to ask God for forgiveness for our sins, and we needed to ask Him personally to help us with our child.

Hesitantly, my husband agreed to pray with me. Since then, we've verbalized all our prayers to Jesus every night.

Praying together with my husband was the right start but I remembered the Bible also speaks of doing penance for sins. I remembered the story of the people of Nineveh putting on sack clothes and ashes for penance.

> When the people of Nineveh believed God; they proclaimed a fast, and all of them, great and small, put on sackcloth When God saw by their actions how they turned from their evil way, he repented of the evil that he had threatened to do to them; he did not carry it out. (Jonah 3:5, 10)

I knew ashes and sack clothes were not appropriate these days, but I was driven to find some way to do penance for my sins. Fasting was not an option because I needed all of my strength. I contemplated how I would demonstrate penance,[1] and decided that I would take my showers with cold water every night until God heard me and fixed my oldest child.[2] For a long time I didn't tell my husband about this small, daily penance. I knew he would not understand. What mattered most was that God knew of, and understood, my penance. He would hear me.

Every night, for a month or two, I took a cold shower. I pleaded, "God, please fix my kids! Fix my oldest one! You fixed the blind and

---

[1] Matthew 6:16–18 "When you fast, do not look gloomy like the hypocrites. They neglect their appearance, so that they may appear to others to be fasting. Amen I say to you, they have received their reward. But when you fast, anoint your head and wash your face, so that you may not appear to be fasting, except to your Heavenly Father who is hidden. And your Father who sees what is hidden will repay you."

[2] Leviticus 9:7 Moses said to Aaron, "Come to the altar and sacrifice your sin offering and your burnt offering and make atonement for yourself and the people; sacrifice the offering that is for the people and make atonement for them, as the LORD has commanded."

the deaf! You can fix this!" I prayed for forgiveness for everything that I had done or said wrong.[3] I apologized to God for whatever my family had done wrong.[4] I completely accepted the blame.[5] I was desperate. I placed all of my trust in God to help me. I prayed so much for my oldest child, asking God to give me her pain.

I did receive pain.

During the day I was cheerful, but in the evenings, life was different. As I got ready for bed a terrible loneliness would encompass me. I would ask my husband to please hold me because I felt so alone. It was as though I were in hell.

One evening I woke up in the middle of the night to feed the baby. I felt sad because of the problems with my oldest. I went to get the bottle and fed the baby. I prayed and cried with my entire heart looking up and saying, "All you saints up there. Tell God. I don't know! I don't know what to do!"

When I'd finished praying, I felt done — as though I'd said it all. I went back to bed and felt at peace. A few days before, I had quit taking my cold showers. I had originally thought I would stop the penance when everything was resolved. However, I quit because I felt as though I did not need to do any more penance. I felt finished.

Surprise

Several days later, I had a strange experience driving home after dropping my second oldest child off at preschool. Hovering about thirty feet above the road there was a very straight neon orange line of light. It did not appear to be attached to anything so I looked harder at it as my car approached. I tried to focus my eyes to see

---

[3] Nehemiah 9:1,2 On the twenty-fourth day of the same month, the Israelites gathered together, fasting and wearing sackcloth and having dust on their heads. 2 Those of Israelite descent had separated themselves from all foreigners. They stood in their places and confessed their sins and the wickedness of their fathers.

[4] Deuteronomy 5:8–9 "You shall not make for yourself an idol in the form of anything in heaven above or on the earth beneath or in the waters below. You shall not bow down to them or worship them; for I, the LORD your God, am a jealous God, punishing the children for the sin of the fathers to the third and fourth generation of those who hate me."

[5] James 4:10 Humble yourselves before the Lord and he will exalt you.

what it was. The light had what looked like heat energy coming out of it and it was pulsing on both ends, but I could see no real end. I thought to myself, "What is that?" I glanced in my rearview mirror to see if the man in the pickup behind me saw the light. It looked as though he saw nothing. I looked ahead again and the line of light started coming down towards the car. I slowed but knew I couldn't stop because the pickup might rear-end me. The light continued descending and hit my windshield with a loud bang!

I was startled! I looked in my rearview mirror again, wondering whether the man in the pickup saw what had just happened! He looked as though he had seen nothing! I was shaken, as though I'd just been in a wreck. It was worse than a wreck because I could not see a trace of anything on the road and the windshield looked fine. It was so strange! I considered turning the car around to look for evidence of what hit me. I was too startled. I kept driving. When I arrived home I told my husband what had happened. He checked the car but found no damage and went back to work. I was perplexed. I took my two year old from the car and went back to work. This event happened right before the next surprise that I received.

FIRST MORE PROBLEMS

I found large amounts of hair under the couch and under a bed! It was my oldest daughter's hair! She pulled her hair out! It was so bad that she had a bald spot and an open wound on her scalp. I was frightened! I told her to leave it alone but she continued to scratch it daily.

I took her to the doctor for treatment. He examined her and was very concerned with what he saw. He didn't exactly tell me what he was thinking but after a long pause he told me to try something. He suggested I start using positive reinforcement as much as possible to get her to leave the wound alone. He told me to give her a reward for leaving the wound on her head alone and gradually increase the number of days between the rewards. This seemed to help a little but there were still so many problems.

A SECOND SURPRISE

A few days later I was taking a shower when I received another surprise. A voice spoke in my heart. The words were, **"Did you get**

my gift?" I thought to myself, "I've heard of listening to your heart but I never thought I would hear an actual voice in my heart." A few years prior to this I had practiced trying to follow my heart and intuition but this was new and different! Reviewing the words and the voice, I wondered if the question could be referring to the doctor's positive reinforcement idea or might be about the light that hit the car. Both of these events did not seem to be helpful enough to fix the problems. I continued to ponder the words and realized that the question needed to be answered. My mind couldn't think of anything, however. Then my heart answered all by itself, saying, **"Yes, but not much."** I was startled again! I reviewed the conversation a few times with amazement. After what seemed like a few seconds, the voice came to my heart once more and said, **"There's more coming."** I questioned over and over, "There's more coming? What? There's more coming?" I reviewed the entire conversation, never fully understanding its meaning. Finally I accepted that there was more coming. I thought, "Okay, there's more coming."

The following days I was quieter, much quieter. I helped my children instead of correcting them all the time. My focus was not on problems, probably because I was still in awe, wondering and questioning. I rarely spoke. This was a new way of acting for me that I had not considered. My mind kept turning back to wondering about this "more" that was coming.

After pondering for a few days, the voice **spoke** to me in a different way and said, **"Do what you wouldn't do."** [6 7 8 9 10 11 12] I thought about this message and what it was that I wouldn't do.

---

[6] Rom 12:20 "Rather, if your enemy is hungry, feed him; if he is thirsty, give him something to drink; for by so doing you will heap burning coals upon his head." Do not be conquered by evil but conquer evil with good.

[7] Deuteronomy 10:18 He defends the cause of the fatherless and the widow, and loves the alien, giving him food and clothing.

DO WHAT YOU WOULDN'T DO?

What a perplexing statement. I tried all kinds of things at first. I tried to choose clothes without opinion. I would just look in the closet and put on whatever my eyes came to. I decorated my home and found that plaids or stripes could actually be complementary to prints. I had never noticed nor thought of that blend of patterns. Soon I evaluated the value decorating had on the problems. It was not the solution, but these were the first few earnest steps toward the ultimate answer. Taking these steps was okay, but I had to find out exactly what He wanted me to do.

Checking Priorities

Videos and TV

One day, I noticed that my daughter was acting like the human-like animal in a famous children's movie. She was yelling at me from the top of the stairs in a very gruff voice. I'd always monitored the things that my children watched and carefully chosen videos to purchase. I did not allow the kids to watch violent shows but we did buy "typical" kid's shows. I kept cartoon videos that had a few angry, selfish, grumpy or loud characters. I thought, if the ending had a good moral, a small amount of "evil" in the video was acceptable. My

---

[8] Proverbs 3:5–6 Trust in the Lord with all your heart, on your own intelligence rely not; in all your ways be mindful of him, and he will make straight your paths.

[9] Jeremiah 29:11 "For I know well the plans I have for you," says the Lord, "plans for your welfare, not for woe! Plans to give you a future full of hope."

[10] Luke 17:33 "Whoever seeks to preserve his life will lose it, but whoever loses it will save it."

[11] Ruth 2:11–12 Boaz replied, "I've been told all about what you have done for your mother-in-law since the death of your husband—how you left your father and mother and your homeland and came to live with a people you did not know before. May the LORD repay you for what you have done. May you be richly rewarded by the LORD, the God of Israel, under whose wings you have come to take refuge."

[12] Genesis 12:1, 4–5 God told Abram: "Leave your country, your family, and your father's home for a land that I will show you." So Abram left just as God said, and Lot left with him. Abram was seventy-five years old when he left Haran. Abram took his wife Sarai and his nephew Lot with him, along with all the possessions and people they had gotten in Haran, and set out for the land of Canaan and arrived safe and sound.

daughter's behavior made me question this belief. I searched for other videos that had anger or fighting in them. I pulled them from the drawer and stored them in the garage, with the intent of getting rid of them. I could not get rid of the videos yet. My husband would not agree. I told him about the few actions I had discovered which were similar to shows the children had watched. I told him, "I'm only removing the videos with anger or meanness." He thought, then disagreed saying, "That will be almost everything." I held back by saying, "Okay. What we can do, is edit the spots where the characters are doing mean things or talking mean. Do you think you can do that?" He really didn't like that idea very much but I remained composed as though he was not frustrated and questioned, "Which videos do you want in the house first?" I gave him a few ideas saying, "These here have only a few mean locations that could use editing. It shouldn't take very long." He agreed to start editing and later I took over. Some of the videos had so much violence or anger it was not worth editing them. Those we got rid of.

From that time on we took a careful approach to all television viewing.

Although some of the children resisted and questioned our motives, we said we'd bring home new videos to replace the old ones. The new peaceful videos helped the children realize we were trying to do what was best for them. Our family watched these recordings often. The children's behavior improved after a few weeks of viewing the revised movies.

Months later the entire family's views were crystallized when we were watching a cartoon video about the Good Samaritan. This video actually showed the traveler being beaten by the robbers. Immediately after seeing this, my two-year-old son started to hit my husband, just like in the video. Needless to say, we don't own that video anymore.

Over time, the older kids have seen that people are influenced by what they view and listen to. They are pretty much the monitors for television because of their concern for each other. They realized that what people see goes into the mind and the heart. We want to keep our minds and hearts pure.[13]

[13] Ephesians 5:10–13 Find out what pleases the Lord. Have nothing to do with the fruitless deeds of darkness, but rather expose them. For it is shameful even to mention what the disobedient do in secret. But everything exposed by the light becomes visible.

WHAT ELSE WOULDN'T I DO?

Books

It is very important for children to learn from books also, and I knew that children learn not just facts but any reaction or attitude expressed in them.

I looked at characters in books.

There were problems between characters in books. Many had a few problems occur in the storyline. My decision was to get rid of some, change the wording in others and use the same wording in others with a change in the tone of the voices.

WHAT ELSE WOULDN'T I DO?

Stuff

A mutual decision was made to clear out the things we did not need. The work load decreased and the house felt freer.

I was ready to do anything.

WHAT ELSE WOULDN'T I DO?

Notice and Attempt Change

In this questioning state, I looked at everything in a new way. Every day something deeply impressed me. I viewed kind, loving, and gentle actions that others used. Reviewing the actions mentally, I was set to display them when the chance came that day. I considered the actions as though I had never really seen or heard of them. I applied one each day.[14]

Over the course of many days, I noticed:
- people who commented on their child's eyes or their hands.
- someone get down to eye level and talk to his or her child.
- how careful some people were when they picked up or put down their child.
- people saying sweet things to babies.
- kind words.

---

[14] Romans 13:14 Rather, clothe yourselves with the Lord Jesus Christ, and do not think about how to gratify the desires of the sinful nature.

- smiles that expressed love.
- someone holding both hands of their child and talking kindly with them to get their full attention.
- a forehead being kissed.
- a child's hair being stroked.
- pats on the back.
- people who earnestly talked as though they wanted to help when others had problems.
- encouraging words.
- high-fives.
- sweet inflections in voices.

After a few weeks the voice told me, **"You don't know how to love right."** Surprisingly, perhaps, I was thankful to hear that. At least I knew my problem now, right? Later that evening I happily told my husband what the voice had said. He was listening and typing on the computer. As soon as I spoke, the voice spoke again, and said, **"You have so much more to learn."** I was surprised and *thankful* to hear that too.

Later the voice said, **"You have eyes and you do not see and you have ears and you do not hear."** This took me by surprise, because I truly did love God and cared about others. I had been struggling so hard all my life in attempt to follow all of the commandments. How could what I heard be true? I did not understand but I thankfully accepted the words as truth.

I continued to notice more things. I saw:
- parents proudly speaking of their child's small accomplishments.
- parents who earnestly appreciated their children's artwork.
- parents who put their children in classes such as ballet, art, cooking, etc.
- parents who allowed their children to experiment and make mistakes.
- patience.
- parents who made things for their children.
- parents holding their child's hand while they walked.
- parents who trusted their older children with their baby.
- a woman who carefully and quietly set down her glass.

- a book that asked children about their interests.
- people who read to their older children.
- people who were very personable.
- people who were brave.
- people who liked math and talked highly of school.
- people who were accepting of others.
- people who were helpful.
- parents taking pictures of their baby being wonderful and trying new things.
- people hugging children for being wonderful and playing nicely.
- a person who said "thank you" frequently, sweetly and right away.
- someone saying "thank you" when something was done correctly.
- someone looking sweetly into their child's eyes and talking with the child.
- teenagers so interested in their sweetheart that they watched everything they did as though it was the best thing ever.
- people working together and developing plans in order to get everyone to want the same goal.
- a child character in a book become less controlling. I noticed the reaction of the other characters.
- someone getting a backrub.
- people who were in a hurry yet patient in line at the store.
- a parent who was nice to a child who had been hurt and also nice to the child who had hurt the other child.
- people who forgave as though the problem were no problem at all.
- people who talked of their children's strengths.
- someone who was very logical.

For a while longer I was drawn to notice certain kind actions. I waited to administer the particular action to my oldest child.

I rocked my baby. I smiled at my baby. I thought, "Okay, I'll try that on my oldest too."

It was very busy around the house and there were very few things that pleased me about the actions of my oldest child. I patiently waited for the right moment when it would be possible to deliver the action and/or the kind words. I knew the moment would come; I believed it would come. It was like having a chore to do, somewhat like folding the laundry. A person holds the chore in the back of their mind and just has to believe and focus on finding time to do it. I believed that God would give the chance to do the job. I was patient and looked for the opportunity. Patience and sincere waiting allowed me to see the moment arrive.

I expected to see something easy to do each day. My attention seemed to drift to what God wanted me to notice in others. I would copy the good I had seen from others in the past few months. Occasionally, there was an easier day. On the easy days the idea was just given to me. Then I'd have more days of searching and being alone. It seemed I was left to live life by myself. "Had I done something wrong?" I prayed questioning God deeply, "What did I do to make you leave? Where did you go? I'm sorry. Please, continue to help me. I don't know what to do." I got no answer. So I went back to doing the things I'd seen and done before. I remembered and redid many of those actions. These times, I noticed the responses from my children.

Children Learn Touch

Roughness
My daughter was rough with other children.

Gentleness Shows Love
One morning I woke to the idea "only touch her very softly." Sitting on the front stairs I'd place my hand on the back of her shoulder ever so softly while waiting for our car pool. I did this for three to four weeks.

Gentleness Teaches Love
One morning I was helping the other children when my eldest came up and touched me on the shoulder so softly. It startled me because I recognized the action as my own. I realized, "Touch is learned!"

Praying for others

I felt sorry for others whom I could see having difficulties with their children. I know I had lots of problems, but I still feared for others. I did not want them to go through the terrible times I'd seen. My children had improved a little already and I did not feel so bothered or angry. God had not spoken or been close by for quite some time now (maybe a few months). I asked Him why He hadn't helped me — why He was staying so far away. Then my prayer changed.

I prayed for others. I told God, "It's not fair, people don't know what they are doing." I asked, "Please, you've got to send someone." It was still. In the quietest voice I heard, "Okay. You." These words startled and frightened me. I thought, "I know nothing." After that I could not deny what I had heard. I just remembered...

I still wanted God to help me. I wanted Him to speak to me and tell me He was okay with me. I did not get that kind of answer. He said, "I'll talk to you again, someday." That answer wasn't what I'd hoped for, however I concluded He was not angry and that was enough to make me happy.

WHAT WOULDN'T I DO NOW?

.... a response.?

One afternoon, one of my younger children wanted someone to play with her. None of the other kids wanted to play. My thought was, "What wouldn't I do now?" Normally cooking was a priority. This time I turned off the stove, set the pan aside and played with the left-out child. The other kids wanted to play too. I knew, "They're copying me. I can teach them different, better actions."

My good action revealed the real reason I should be helping. If I truly cared, I would have to take steps to make a difference. Real love takes action. I'd been teaching my children inaction and selfishness.

The kids acted in so many undesirable ways because of me! Knowing this did not feel good. I felt weighted with GUILT.

How do I get rid of this guilt?

The only consolation was in knowing the children had followed the example set in the recent cooking episode. I questioned wholeheartedly, "Could all be mended? I loved the children. Trust in God would have to keep fear and worry away daily. The decision would be to look forward to the path out of this.

I had hope. I knew what I wanted more than anything: I wanted only love in our home.

For months I searched deep into my actions and motives. This was hard. I was torn when I saw poor reactions from the children. I hated those actions. I wanted to believe it was okay for me to act grouchy, label someone in anger, or to strike out. I believed in these actions. The kids just had to be stopped. I wanted to get away. I didn't know how to respond.

With a little more thought I remembered the phrase, "People act like who their God is." I knew God is great in power, full of love, abounding in kindness, slow to anger, gracious, compassionate, forgiving, and forgets our sins. I compared my reactions to how God responds. My actions and attitudes could not compare to these good attributes.

I desired to act in God's ways because I loved my children. The destruction I'd seen showed me the road I'd been following. In the past, I acted morally only because I wished to go to heaven. Now, I decided, I needed to change that. I would act morally because it was God's will, not to obtain anything for myself. That's what God wanted from me. I tried to be more like Jesus and learn kindness and love from Him. God had to show me. When I asked God a question, or to help me, I learned to expect an answer, even if it wasn't necessarily the one I had in mind. When I asked God for things, I would often voice my prayer like this, "God, please help me find a way to [____] if it is your will." I knew that God, our father, would help me by giving what I needed.

Luke 11:13 "If you then, though you are evil, know how to give good gifts to your children, how much more will your Father in Heaven give the Holy Spirit to those who ask him!"

ATTEMPTING TO ACT LIKE JESUS...

I tried to talk calmly to my baby at all times. If she wanted something that was not good for her, I would say "no" very calmly as many times as she asked. One time I placed her in bed and said, "It's time to go to sleep." She calmly said no several times while I replied yes, just as sweetly. It was so funny. I smiled knowingly and left, saying nicely, "Go to sleep." I remember the understanding I felt and told my husband how she had mirrored my attitude in her speech.

Another day, I saw a wasp, quickly picked up my son and ran away. Later, he exhibited extreme fear of wasps also. Some days later I saw a woman calmly wave her hand to get a wasp off of her food, without saying anything or showing extreme emotion. I decided I would be calm and non-reactive when wasps were around. My demonstration of calmness helped the kids be calmer around bees and wasps.

3
LOVE AND ACTION

Love helped me understand my daughter's feelings. With this understanding and compassion I responded by spending time with her which increased her self-esteem.

Her Heart

As my first and, for a time, only child, the oldest claimed all of my time. She'd always demanded to be talked to and desired to learn. In fact, information was what she always craved.

Our growing family allowed little individual time. The oldest child's choice way to acquire the lost attention was by acting inappropriately. *I* could see that this was illogical, but she was too young to understand.

TAKING STEPS TO HELP

I loved my oldest child and still wanted to teach and spend time with her. I decided to find individual time, even just a few minutes a day, to pay attention to her alone.

She was six years old in first grade and was gone most the day. Before school I would take a few minutes to teach her something new.

One morning I taught her how to play jacks. We played a quick game in the afternoon. We tried other games and crafts (such as string games, marbles clapping songs, stitching, etc.) I also asked her questions regarding her favorite things which increased familiarity and enjoyment between us. Over the course of months she learned as many things as I could think to teach her. The new information, positive rewards, along with the increased interaction created a happier child due to an increase in self esteem. By and by she stopped the self-destructive behavior. I noticed that other parents often enrolled their children in dance, gymnastics, or art classes at the recreation center. I knew little about such activities, but decided to allow her to try them. She enjoyed the classes. It seemed this was a stimulation she needed. The classes opened her mind to new things and heightened her interest in new areas. She became interested in everything she was a part of. However, there was still a problem with parts of her attitude. In response, I looked to see where else she was lacking interaction. The parental interaction that needed improvement was with her father. Then an idea crossed my mind. I would enroll the two of them in activities together. I asked him if I could sign the two of them up for a few classes, including woodworking and astronomy. He agreed heartily because he enjoyed both activities. The classes made it much easier to get acquainted and ensure specific scheduled time where she had his undivided attention.

I Learned Three Things
1. She acquired more self-esteem by learning new things.
2. It opened doors to new interests.
3. The quality time our oldest had with her dad helped establish a bond between them. The relationship with her father was probably what she needed most.

The times were still difficult but the burden was lightened. My focus was changing from looking at and hating the problems to seeing issues, looking in my heart, and asking God to find a time where I could act in a better way.

Actively Finding my Faults

My kids were loud and very hyper. They slammed doors instead of closing them quietly. I saw them moving around so quickly that they were knocking each other down. The kids "took" things from each other instead of asking politely. The root source of this inconsiderate behavior was now obvious. The kids were simply amplifying the speed at which I moved.

- I moved too quickly
- I picked up and put things down very quickly (and ungracefully)
- I allowed doors to slam when I closed them
- I snatched things from my kids without asking
- I did not touch my children gently

I had been focusing singularly on what I needed to get done, with little care about people in my surroundings. I had a flashback to a conversation that I had heard as a child. I remembered hearing that you must pray to find your faults. I also remembered an old book that I had read, that had prompted me to pray to find my faults. The book stated, "Where you have troubles with others, there you will find your faults."

My New Actions

- I needed to keep in mind God's continual presence, even in the children.
- I stopped trying to physically catch my kids to stop them from running in the house.
- I walked slower and I tried to talk more slowly and quietly.
- I slowed down while picking things up.
- I tried to put down my glass at the table slowly and without making any noise.
- I closed doors very slowly.
- I asked my children kindly for an item, then held out the palm of my hand and tapped in the center of my palm to get them to put the item in my hand.
- I once saw someone point and touch the ground and their little toddler sat down. I learned that little children respond well to hand gestures.
- I tried to be very careful and slow when I dressed them. I pulled their shirts over their heads very carefully and gently.
- I walked down the stairs slowly instead of bounding down them.
- I made a point of widening the space between my kids and myself when I walked around them so that I didn't bump into them.

RESULTS

- The older kids were slowing down, a little more careful, and were less hyper.
- My youngest, who was getting older, handled items very carefully. While visiting my mother, my aunt noticed our toddler in the living room picking up a glass globe very carefully and slowly and then setting it down equally as gently. Amazed, she told me how surprised she was that someone so young could be so careful. I knew that my daughter was copying my actions.
- Our youngest showed gentleness and patience with her young cousins too. Asking for a toy she would raise the palm of her hand toward them expecting it to be placed in her hand. The cousin did not recognize the gesture and turned away. Our two-year-old continued to follow the cousin, pointing at her palm. She looked perplexed because her actions weren't working.

When the children followed my new examples, I praised them. When they went back to the old ways, I asked them *nicely* to practice doing it the right way. If they practiced it correctly I'd smile or praise the action. If the action needed a little more work I asked them to practice again possibly five times. Ultimately I'd praise them when the actions were done as correctly as I could expect.

What else wouldn't I do?

DEEPLY EXAMINING MY CONSCIENCE

I carried resentment for the oldest two kids. They didn't listen to me. I'd tell them they had to listen, but force often got more effect than my words. The children were used to being forced to do what they were told.

I knew obedience is more than external.

First: there must be knowledge of laws and expectations.[15]

---

[15] Micah 6:8–9 You have been told, o man, what is good, and what the Lord requires of you: Only to do the right and to love goodness, and to walk humbly with your God. Hark the Lord cries to the city.[It is wisdom to fear your name!]

Second: there should be consequences that are sure to result from failing to follow requests.

Third: there should be forgiveness if the person is sorry and decides to change to obedience.

✳   ✳   ✳

God is our Father, so I had to parent like Him in order to be a fair and just person.

First: I had to be consistent. The expectations should be clear and known to all. Secondly, the consequence should be a logical, easily accessible action that can be carried out.

Second: My actions needed adjustment. The actions were the result of prior beliefs. I had to let go of these incorrect beliefs in order to change in my actions.

The question now consisted of: How should I think and what new way should I act? What actions would cause consistent results (the kids should want to love, obey, and please me)?

Third: I knew I had to react as though I loved each person with whom there was contact. That is how God continually calls us back to him.

Preconceived notions about my kids had to be dropped. Consequently, I learned to look at each individual action and carefully change my response to suit God's ways.

The following tables summarize my beliefs and resulting actions before and after this evaluation.

Before	After
Belief: I will force my kids be good and they will know I've loved them. I will tell them how right I am.	**Belief:** Love the children and they will be glad. They will want to be near and love me.
Action: I will make them talk nicely and share.	**Action:** Let them know the good they do. Speak kindly to them. Share with them.

Before	After
Belief: Children are basically selfish, unkind, uncaring, and or lazy.	**Belief:** God's love is so wonderful that kids will want it if they've experienced it.
Action: Look for their faults. Let them know they are wrong. Punish them for their evil actions.	**Action:** Teach how *good* God's love is. In action be patient, loving, kind, gentle, happy, peaceful, thoughtful, etc.

Before	After
Belief: I know how to do this. I turned out ok. I'll do what worked on me.	**Belief:** I don't know how to respond in every circumstance. I do have guidelines that I will try to keep in place. I will keep my mind open to new ways of speaking. In whatever I do, I believe that if I follow with a caring heart, God will work through me and things will turn out fine. I am able to be a new person now. I'll try to act like God and act like his child. He will show me what I have to do.
Action: Children, I am right. God says you are to be like this so you must be _____.	**Action:** I put on love as the light to follow and use. His simple actions work well.

Before	After
Belief: When something went wrong, I assumed that one of my children was doing something wrong. The child was being selfish or being bad on purpose.	**Belief:** The kids' actions are really are just my belief about them. My kids are good. They need to be taught a new behavior. I let go of preconceived judgments and focused on being a good example.
Actions: I'd judge them. I might tell that what I thought they were like (e.g., selfish) or I'd take things away from them angrily.	**Action:** After their selfish action, I set an example of how to give. I gave them things myself when they asked nicely for it. If they forgot to ask nicely, I would kindly request that they ask nicely. I would do this as many times as needed. When they did ask nicely, I might say "doesn't that make you feel nice" or "that was very nicely said." The new label replaced the old label in both my mind and in their minds.

Before	After
Belief: Faith in my own needs and interests will make me happy. I am able to force happiness. My interests came before my childrens'.	**Belief:** Faith in love allowed me to put my children before myself. I learned that happiness comes from following God.
Actions: I didn't want to be loving or giving at times due to fatigue, stress, or business.	**Action:** I let go of my own troubles. I would do whatever came into my mind in order to help. It was usually simple like patting them on the head or giving them a toy.
Belief: The kids were making me late for important appointments. I blamed them.	**Belief:** It is okay to take the time to be kind even when it doesn't look like there's any time to spare. God will work out everything if I'm doing my best.
Actions: I became stressed and impatient when under time constraints.	**Action:** I logically (without anger) discussed time constraints with my children. I told them to ask me again later if we did not have time to talk at the moment.

Before	After
Belief: I could be a good parent and Christian by making my kids change. Negative reactions would make them feel bad, scared, guilty, or embarrassed enough to change.	**Belief:** I love the kids. I look and see how little they know. I'll trust that they will want God who is all good. I'll teach them how to love properly. They will behave better in the future.
Actions: Using force, anger, hurtful words, guilt trips, and yelling will achieve results.	**Action:** I sought to love my kids all the time. I corrected my own heart. I was unbiased when my children disagreed with me or didn't get along with each other. I was logical. I listened and acknowledged feelings and thoughts. I taught that both individuals are responsible for getting along (when there was a conflict between two children). I required them, in this case, to play well together for a specified time. Praise was given for good behavior. I shared and gave what I normally would not have.

There are two things: wants and needs. God provides needs when trust is put in Him. Wants are vain and don't have value for salvation. They lead away from God. See Ecclesiastes 6: You want what is vain if what you seek is for your body. Vain goals are things people believe they need to produce happiness, such as wealth, fame, attention, possessions, or honor.

Only God can fill our real needs. Hope in Him, because God is the one who cares fully for all people and wants to bless all with good things. His ways are the ways to happiness. He is omnipotent. He knows all our needs. He knows when we can best use his gifts and gives accordingly. He knows if we will use the gift with a pure perspective in mind. (Realize that God is God and that you don't know what is best, see Job 38 and 39.)

Jeremiah 12:11-14 "For I know the plans I have for you," declares the LORD , "plans to prosper you and not to harm you, plans to give you hope and a future. Then you will call upon me and come and pray to me, and I will listen to you. You will seek me and find me when you seek me with all your heart. I will be found by you," declares the LORD, "and will bring you back from captivity. I will gather you from all the nations and places where I have banished you," declares the LORD, "and will bring you back to the place from which I carried you into exile."

Goals that are truly good feed and satisfy the soul with God's goodness, ways, and will. Only God knows what is good for each man in life.

Removing selfishness makes a better parent and a better follower of God. If a person focuses on love and turns to God, He will help them if asked. It's important to realize that God often helps out not when we think we need it, but in his own time, which is exactly the appropriate moment. This focus allows the parent to change into a self giving person, who desires to always spread love.

CHANGE YOUR ATTITUDE

During daily tasks, it's important to look at all actions with an open mind and heart. God will show people what they need to do differently if they are willing to change. Once a person sees the change that needs to be made, he or she should focus on the perfect time to use the better action/attitude. God always provides the opportunity to act correctly and lovingly.

*   *   *

In my experience, my children needed to be taught how to use logic, be patient, and love others. God's peace exhibits these characteristics. I saw the good that came from changing my actions. My children responded to me with love. Over time, I learned how important it is to believe in the power of love. The incredible thing about love and goodness is that it is learned and spread from person to person easily. All it takes is one person's conscious decision to be more loving (more like God) in order to invoke changes in others.

It's especially important to love children and act as though they are inherently good creatures. Since children lack proper understanding of the world around them, mistakes and accidents are inevitable, and it's easy to lose your temper over little things. I often whispered to my kids when they wouldn't listen and spoke calmly when I had to repeat myself. If that didn't work, I often acted as if I were someone else, with various accents or singing. That, surprisingly, got their attention and allowed me to stay calm in the process. Each of my responses that got my children's attention included kindness. It was important for me to remember that logic always works best; I became a new person. Having patience was key for accidental hurts, spills, and repetitive questions, and worked just as well as having a sense of humor. During repetitive questions, I'd ask the child his or her own question. The children learned to answer questions themselves, through logic. Love, kindness and logic were some of the first traits I applied in becoming a new person for my family.

4
MORE TO LEARN & CHANGE

Children Learn Interest

I observed that my oldest child was not interested in her baby sister. She was very busy and acted like she really didn't want to be around either of us. I knew I needed to take time and love my oldest child.

When she was settled in bed and calm, I would talk to her just like I talked to my baby. In a very sweet and cutesy voice I'd say something nice to her. If I had hugged or touched the baby a certain way, I would remember that love around my oldest. I decided to give my oldest more time and love by rocking her (she was a first grader at the time — but as tall as a third or fourth grader).

Eventually, she accepted the touch and didn't try to pull away.

INTEREST TEACHES LOVE

She'd look at me when I was talking to her, and when she did, her eyes began to shine with happiness she hadn't shown in a long time. She took an interest in looking at and holding the baby.

✳   ✳   ✳

Changes

ANGER

For a while, I would spank my kids if I was angry with them. I came to understand, though, that *anger produces retaliation.* The retaliation, amazingly, occurred within the same day! The children would begin to hit each other. They believed that when someone bothered them, the "right" reaction was to hit. I wondered: *If hitting my kids made them hit each other, what would happen if I were more tolerant towards my children?* **I decided to try it.** On days when I did not spank the kids, they didn't hit each other as often. I demonstrated tolerance and consistent patience toward everyone. I tried very hard to find other ways to discipline my children, such as giving them laundry to fold or windows to wash. The hitting decreased.

I still questioned and pondered whether getting rid of the spanking was a good approach. Finally, one day, my thoughts upon this matter were crystallized when my two-year-old saw a fly on the wall and said to me, "Spank him! Make him be bad!" It was very comical, but strangely sad at the same time. I guess I felt guilty because I knew I was the one "making them be bad."

CHILDREN BELIEVE WHAT YOU BELIEVE ABOUT THEM

When my oldest was about six years old, she would not come to me when I called her. She would run away. When I called her to come to dinner, I saw her consciously turn around and run the other way.

Instead of getting frustrated I thought, "I will mention how quickly she is listening to me." When I did this, she looked at me, confused at what I really was getting at. (She seemed to say, "You know I'm not doing the right thing. Why are you praising me?") I kept on saying things about how much I liked her quick reflexes and called to her dad to see it. I continued this approach for several days. She actually got a little better at coming when called.

The problem was not fixed entirely but there was a definite improvement. You see that I was teaching her that I had a new opinion about her. She began to see that I liked her for who she was. Teachers, I have found, have a similar impact on children when they express belief in them.

OBEYING

I tried to exhibit positive expectation when I asked the kids to get off the counter or chairs. I'd point to the ground and ask nicely instead of physically putting the child on the ground and getting irritated. I'd say, "You can ask me to get it for you."

NEATNESS

Our oldest had very poor penmanship. Her assignments were torn and wrinkled. I thought about what positive words could be said about the paper in front of me. *Something I would not normally say?* I saw all of the things that were bad about her paper. I looked for something on the paper that I could praise. I found one letter "e" that was written a little better than the rest of the letters. I absolutely raved about how nice that "e" looked. I mentioned how the letter was written right on the line and its clear form. I continued saying positive things that I wouldn't normally say. I gave her the ideas of becoming a writer, a doctor, a scientist, etc. I, too, decided to write more neatly in order for her to have a good example to copy. I remembered how my dad had told me that he liked the way I left plenty of space between my words. I told this story to my child so that she would copy this in her writing. Over time, her handwriting continued to improve. I continued to use this method with all her work for a couple of years. The improvement was good, but gradual. Today she writes beautifully and gracefully, and is confident in her skill.

Your beliefs about your child are conveyed in your words, tone of voice, actions, attitude, facial expressions, body language, and interest. Children become what you notice about them. If you notice only bad behavior, kids will continue to exhibit this behavior, often in order to get attention. Instead, notice and comment on what they are doing correctly.

Giving attention to a child's good actions fulfills their need to be noticed and praised.

One day I noticed a child whose hug was rejected by another child. A third child saw this and said, "I'll hug you," and she gave the child a hug. I noticed how giving that action was and I knew that her babysitter had displayed that action before. These children were simply "filling the need" in their situation. I decided to try the same technique during other problems. When one of my children would have a problem with a sibling, I would ask the child, "What do you need?" or I would ask, "What can I do?" I noticed my kids would become less angry and stop complaining when I did this. When they understood that I could possibly help them, it was easier for them to solve the original problem.

Filling the need for attention was important when my children got hurt. I would ask them if they needed some ice to put on the bump or bruise. After I had done this several times, one of my kids picked up on it. Whenever someone got hurt, she would run and get ice for the child. The children learned to be logical and "fix the problem" instead of acting illogically, and causing the problem to escalate.

On another occasion, my oldest suddenly decided to disagree with us. In the past, she usually agreed with our viewpoint on appropriate versus inappropriate movies. We had discussed this several times before and she understood the position. She was upset that her friends watched shows that she could not and felt that our viewpoint was incorrect. I thought that I should "do what I wouldn't do" and I asked her to tell me how I should handle this situation. I asked, without anger and encouraged her to say whatever she wanted to say. She told me that I was wrong. I asked her if she really meant what she was saying. I asked her if I should change the way I was handling movies and TV. She thought, and then changed her mind. I shouldn't change the way I was handling it. She told me that it was hard to be different from her friends. I realized that she just wanted to express her frustration. I needed to continue to be a good listener, letting her express her feelings. I was, "filling the need" for my daughter in this situation.

After having witnessed the success of "filling the need," I used this solution outside of my immediate family. If someone was having a problem or a family needed help, I would try to follow up and fill the need in that person's life. Actively responding to other's important needs (not wants), I started to listen to God's voice in my heart, especially when I was called to help others. Any small act towards an individual, even the offer alone, provided help. Whenever it was possible, I strove to help others with their problems.

ATTENTION

My second child demanded attention for small hurts or injuries. We decided to be extra caring when she got hurt or felt poorly. If she was hurt, we hurried to get her some ice and, if she felt ill, we would have her lay her head on our shoulder or get a pillow for her. When she was cold we'd get her a blanket. We were implementing the "Do what you wouldn't do" technique. After a few weeks of this behavior, we heard that she had exhibited a behavior similar to our own. She let her friend put her head on her shoulder all the way home from summer camp because her friend had a migraine headache.

I treated all the children equally (attention, gifts, etc.) and tried to fill large gaps if others did not act so equally. These people often included grandparents, relatives, and friends.

It is important that each parent gives attention, talks to, does things with, and connects with each child, otherwise behavioral problems (stubbornness, uncaring, crying, and the inability to get along with other children) may arise. Children also copy the emphasis a parent places on equality. Children are very capable of learning to give attention to people who need it most.

POSITIVE FEELINGS FROM SUCCESS

My fourth child, while in an art class, was given attention by the art teacher, who asked questions and noticed some bright colors and detail. The instructor also mentioned, "It is vital for the children not only to attempt but to feel successful concerning their work." She repeated the entire project in order for all of the students to achieve their goal. Again, I saw that speech should focus on the desired results.

Experience proved to me that young children *don't listen* if you tell them *not* to do something.

Here are some examples of my fifth child behaving in the way she was told not to.

We read a book in which the main character went to an art museum and saw modern art (scribbles on the canvas). Later, the character went home and drew scribbles on her white walls. I told my five-year-old child, who had never written on walls before, that the character should not have written on the walls. Several days later my child wrote on our walls. I gave her a wash rag and a little cleanser to get the writing off the walls. A few days later she did it again. She willingly cleaned it up again. I continued to be nice to her. She stopped after the second attempt. I figured that she was just trying out a new idea that had never occurred to her before, even though we had discussed the action and concluded that it wasn't acceptable. It was amazing to me that she copied the action even though I told her, "Don't do it."

On another occasion, my sister, who was visiting our house, told me about one of her kids cutting her own hair. I'd never had that problem before. Since I already knew that children like to try new things, I looked around to see if my daughter was listening. She didn't look affected in any way, so I let the anxiety pass. Some days later, the same child tried cutting her own hair.

I learned three lessons:
1. Children will try new things they hear or see.
2. Children are not logical (but that doesn't mean that they're "bad").
3. Children are always listening.

A Question

I knew my little child was good and meant well. I wondered why she performed the actions in the previous two stories. Was it because I'd mentioned the action the child shouldn't be doing? Is that the problem? Then I thought, "How can I parent at all if I can't tell my child what's not acceptable?" For several weeks I tried to figure out how to change bad behavior without mentioning the bad behavior (i.e., "don't do this").

5
LEARNING TO SPEAK POSITIVELY

Trusting

I thought, "God will show me. He helps people with their problems."

An Answer

Soon after putting trust in God, I spoke to a dental hygienist during a regular dental visit. She mentioned how some children are afraid of the dentist office. These children act in a variety of ways such as wildness, nervousness, being fearful, etc. She said, "It's no wonder they react that way. The parents make them afraid. They say, 'If you don't brush your teeth you'll get cavities.'" I had used those words myself. I hid my guilt and questioned, "What should they say?"

She replied, "They could say something like this: 'If you brush your teeth regularly you will protect your teeth.'"

Pondering...

After that dental visit, I analyzed the lady's statement for days. What made that wording so much better than the other wording?...

Discovery

I discovered there is a positive way to say something and a negative way. Positive speech focuses on the good you want and the benefit of the correct action. Positive speech encourages more good behavior. Negative speech works by fear, focuses on what you don't like or want. Negative statements cause fear, anger, resentment, worry, despair and low self-esteem. I came up with a saying, which my oldest daughter took a liking to, "If you tell someone, 'Don't think about a pink and purple spotted elephant,' what do you think they will think about?" She agreed that saying what you didn't want nearly forced the person to do what you didn't want. If one were to say instead, "Think of a blue tiger," the person would never think of the elephant.

A conclusion

Positive statements must be more effective to modify behavior than negative statements because they point to a *way out*, a solution. Positive statements believe in a good outcome.

Speaking positively required a lot of concentration. To get a very positive sentence, I had to break down all the words to check if the sentence needed revising. Thus I regularly found myself speaking and then revising the wording to be as positive as I could. See the section "Staying Positive" for examples and suggestions for positive speech.

As mentioned, positive speech is especially important for young children. Young children hear action words and diligently perform them. They are not logical and do not always process every word, even if you're emphasizing not to do something. Reminding children is okay, but remember to notice good memory in children as often as possible.

Chapter 9, "Key Learnings" has many more examples of how to say things positively.

6

CHILDREN LEARN FROM EACH PARENT

Children learn to act kindly to siblings and friends if their parents are consistently kind to them.

Anger in Competition

My children became very frustrated when they played games and lost. They were very competitive. Our kids copied not only my behavior, but the behavior of their father. Losing board games bothered him. Three of our kids often acted very tense, like my husband. I decided that the ultra-competitive behavior had to stop because it was causing fights between the children. The arguing continued during the games even when the children were asked to play nicely and talk politely to each other. Positive words were not enough to change the behavior this time.

Modeling

I asked my husband to play games with the children and allow himself to lose purposefully and cheerfully at the same time. He modeled very well.

Result

The kids picked up on being better losers. They were having much more fun playing games together.

More Results

Weeks later, my boy, who had already won several races in track, saw that one of his friends had no 1st place ribbons yet. He actually slowed down and let his friend win the last race so he could win a blue ribbon.

More Play

Another day, I observed my son playing with toy cars. While playing, he slammed the cars together very roughly. I knew that neither my husband nor I had modeled this behavior. I thought, "He must have picked it up from TV or from other kids."

Modeling

Since he seemed to more closely emulate his father's behavior, I asked Dad to play cars with our son and play very carefully. My husband took one of my son's airplanes and showed him how to play very carefully and slowly with it.

Result

After about two sessions, my son played much more gently with his toys.

Girls Playing

In the meantime, my girls played with dolls. I noticed that they acted selfishly, frequently resulting in fights. I used the modeling idea on the girls, focusing on being polite and kind while playing. I asked my kids, "Do you mind if I wear those shoes?" or "Would it be okay if my doll did this?" I also said nice things like "Oh, that's cute!"

Result

After a couple of sessions, my positive modeling helped the girls play nicer together.

Conclusion

Some of our children were like me, and others were like my husband. I believed that the parent whose personality relate most to the child would be most effective to model a new behavior

At first I wanted to change my child to fix the problems. After doing many of the things discussed already, I realized that I had been changing myself, and just as easily decreasing the problems. The process seemed to be: change myself first and then the child will copy the behavior.

Problem

There was a problem with this approach, however, which continually put a glitch in the process. The glitch came from my husband not behaving in the way I wanted the children to act. At this point, I wasn't quite sure what to do, but I was very concerned because three of our five children most closely emulated him.

7

NEW CHAPTER IN OUR LIVES

A few months before our fifth child was born, God sent me another message. It was a thought that was true. The message was, "Joy is coming."

How was I supposed to know what that meant? It just helped me believe that the family would become happy soon. How soon? I didn't know. Was the baby the joy?

God Showed Us How to Love AGAIN

The baby that did arrive was so easy to take care of and love. She is always happy. She did bring lots of joy and understanding of how to love. All the children learned from her presence.

A few years after the baby was born we decided to move in closer to other families to make it easier for playmates to visit.

The move must have been sent from above because we found a house that fit us so perfectly. The move went so smoothly, etc.

The Process Started Again

So, let's check our priorities again...

SIMPLIFY AGAIN

Before moving into our new home, my husband had a choice to make. All of his woodworking equipment, which was previously kept in its own shed, needed a spot for itself in the new home. We decided that it would have to go into the garage, but it was a tight fit. I told my husband that he could build a new shop, but also asked him what he would make. We didn't need any more cabinets for our house. I suggested that he could make cabinets for others. He considered this, and thought about adding onto the existing garage. Adding on, though, cost more than we were willing to pay. Instead, my husband decided to sell his equipment in an attempt to focus his time and effort on his family. That made me very happy.

Once he sold the equipment, my husband told me that he felt as though a great weight had been lifted from his shoulders. He didn't have to worry about his hobby anymore and he was happy to spend more time with the children and me.

At the same time, also we gave away of a lot of "stuff" that we had in the house. We got rid of toys, pictures, books, games, clothing, jewelry, and many other items we didn't need or use often. The more "stuff" we got rid of, the better the house felt. I even got rid of home decorations. Our focus changed from acquiring things, to more family times, and loving God and our kids. I realized the accumulation of too many belongings caused unnecessary stress and took my mind off what was really important in life.

I was the main driver of this process for the first six years. My husband let me do these things, but was not a particularly active participant. He would do what I asked him to, but I was afraid of asking too often because he wouldn't make changes on his own. Despite this, he was always helpful and accepting of me. There was a distinct difference between my husband's actions and mindset and my own. It was obvious to me that a few of the kids acted like me while the others took to him more easily.

QUARRELLING AND LACK OF ATTENTION

A problem soon erupted between our two eldest children.

The quarreling continued mostly because I sided with the younger child who had my personality, while my husband sided with the older child who had his disposition. My husband and I agreed to become neutral during the disputes that arose between these two girls. Neither of us gave any indication of which side we agreed with, but rather loved both children and helped them solve the disputes. The problem really belonged to both of them because they both contributed to it. Our solution was for both children to practice getting along for a period of say, ten minutes every time they had an argument.

The second reason for the quarreling also needed to be addressed. My husband's interest in our oldest daughter's life left our second daughter with little interest from her father. I tried to give her extra time, but I could not make up for the lack of attention given her. Finally, I asked him to purposely ask questions and become more aware of the younger girl's friends and interests. The oldest girl became more accepting and friendly with her sister after my husband showed by his actions that our second daughter had interests that mattered. The older child even started drawing Anime like the younger. Now the younger of the two is working diligently to make herself a better basketball player, like my oldest daughter.

My husband shifted his attention to all the kids and everyone gets along much better now.

To help increase how much the kids were getting along I took photos and talked about how much fun they were having. The pictures were put on display to reinforce the fact that they did have fun together. Soon, the children got along more often, which provided opportunities for me to comment on good behavior and take more photos.

Eventually, our two oldest daughters started having in-depth conversations which my husband and I encouraged by our interest and involvement.

The two girls are best friends today. My oldest daughter is getting ready to enter her senior year in high school and is looking at colleges that she wants to attend. Her sister, a sophomore, has expressed a desire to keep her sister close to home many times because they are such good friends.

QUARRELING AND NEGATIVE ATTENTION

Negative attention can be just as detrimental to the desired behavior as no attention whatsoever.

I noticed that our son was not getting along with our oldest child. In this case I could see that the disparity between the two children was due to the fact that our son found the older sibling's actions to be annoying. I noticed the exact time where he learned this behavior. It occurred during dinner, the same time that her father was critical of her eating habits. He was copying his father!

In order to fix this problem, my husband made distinct efforts to be positive when talking to the oldest child at dinner and to be more polite during dinner himself.

We wanted the oldest child to think, also, that our son was worth playing with, so her father played with his son where the oldest was free to observe the action. A few days later, I distinctly remember seeing the two kids playing together with Legos. I greeted my husband at the front door after he came home from work and quietly pointed out the sound of kids happily playing upstairs. From that time forward, the two of them have gotten along much better.

DISAPPROVAL CAUSES PROBLEMS

Children believe what you believe about them…remember!

The main frustration that my husband still had with our oldest child was her lack of basketball skills. Sometimes it made him angry at her. He would even keep a tally of how many times a mistake happened. His focus was on the negative mistakes rather than the positive accomplishments. This resulted in much frustration for him and poor self-esteem (and athletic performance) for her. I had a thought, "A toddler learning to walk is praised even when they only walk a few steps and then fall down. Parents do not focus on how many times a baby falls or even teeters." I gave my husband this example and politely asked him to offer only positive comments and encouragement to tell her what he liked about what she was doing. I wanted him to do this even if she tried something new and failed.[16] He tried positive comments such as, "I saw you thinking about taking the ball to the hoop when you were at the foul line." This kind of wording was a good way to stay positive and encourage at the same time.

---

[16] 1 Peter 3:1-2 Likewise, you wives, should be subordinate to your husbands so that, even if some disobey the word, they may be won over without a word by their wives' conduct when they observe your reverent and chaste behavior.

He decided that he'd only praise her and offer encouragement to try new things.

If she had negative feelings about how she had played the game, he would listen and acknowledge her feelings, but move back into positive territory quickly. Of course, he still wished she would improve. He would talk to her about trying something new at another time, when she was calmer. His positive wording had so much effect that our daughter became more accepting of his ideas. Self-esteem improved, she stopped picking on siblings, became more relaxed, and had a better attitude on the basketball floor.

Finally, we began to see major improvements in our oldest girl. I was *so thankful!* I thanked God for his help. I was also thankful to my husband for trying new things. All our relationships increased in love. We also noticed our daughter being more helpful with peers since Dad was only giving out help

Looking back on all that happened, sometimes I think God must have been slowly changing me and helping and preparing my husband to make similar changes.

At this point, my husband had let go of his wants in order to focus on understanding others.

AH, BUT WE WERE STILL HAVING SOME PROBLEMS...

I was internally bothered that my husband was continuing to make mistakes with the kids. He did not realize what he was doing. I finally couldn't stand it any longer. I did tell him; I told him in the morning.

He was just waking up, so I said peacefully, "You know how I care about you. I know you have been doing whatever I ask you specifically to do. But, you need to do more. Some dads smile at their kids. Some dads pick them up or pat them on the back and notice them. Some dads laugh at cute things they say or do. I want you to be like that."

I began sobbing. I told him some of the things that he needed to do (talk nicely all the time, love being their dad, etc.) to be a better parent. This was extremely difficult for me to say because I'd always talked to him about what I loved about him. We never argued. I knew he always listened to me so I hoped that he would hear what I had to say.

For a few minutes, my husband rejected what I told him. He didn't think he had a problem.

He retorted, "I've been doing a lot! How many other men listen to their wives like I do?"

I said, "Well they've been good changes haven't they? Don't you think things are improving? I've just been telling you little things to do. I don't ever yell at you or get mad at you, but I feel so angry at you when you sound so unhappy or get angry about little things all the time. You never laugh! You're never really happy! When I was about to get married to you, I told my mom my concern. She said you would be happy when we got married. I want you to be happy with the kids. I know you love me. Please."

He sat stiffly at the edge of the bed with his back toward me.

I said, "Don't be mad."

He raised his hand in order to say, "Please stop talking. I need to consider this for a moment."

It was very quiet in the room. He laid his head on his hand. I was afraid I'd hurt his feelings.

Then he said, "You're saying I'm a bad dad."

"No. You're a good dad. You've been helping in the house. You've been making things better with the kids. You help when I need it. If you could just not let everything bother you..."

He was quiet again. Then he said, "What do you want me to do?"

I came from behind him and hugged him. I said, "If you could just not be so angry when things go wrong, I would be happier. If someone spills their drink, just have them wipe it up. If you have trouble opening something don't grumble, just try something else. Don't let little things bother you. Do not let all the things that don't work out around you accumulate; when they are over, forget them."

He warmed up to the suggestions.

LESS INTENSE

Initially, in the next few days, when he was bothered by the kids he would just say nothing. This was an important step because he was critical of the kids in many things. He did not like it when things went wrong.

Next, I asked him to look on the bright side at all times. This was tough for him, but he started to say some happier sentences.

If it rained he might say, "It's raining. Well, the plants needed it."

If there was no time to do what he wanted, he might say, "Well, it must not have been the right time to do it. There must be a good reason."

Eventually I tried to show him that good things continued to happen, even though they may have looked like bad things initially.

Weeks later I asked him to try and be more cheerful, happy, and smiling. Breakfast time was a good time to start this. Breakfast had always been sullen. I thought it would be good for the kids to start the day out with some happiness.

The kids were not able to laugh at themselves because my husband would not laugh at himself or laugh at all when something went wrong (which was almost all the time). I asked my husband to be less intense and to laugh when things went wrong instead of getting mad about it. I wasn't telling him to laugh just because things went wrong but I wanted him to lighten up and be easier going. It was so the kids would follow his example.

He started to lighten the mood at breakfast by talking about things, using a little humor, hugging the kids, patting them on the back, and saying nice things about how they looked or acted. In a short time, breakfast, and the rest of the day, became more fun for everyone.

By doing these things, the children were able to deal with problems better, get along more, the amount of problems decreased, and the overall mood lightened. Getting ready in the morning was easier. My husband told me that by being less intense, it was easier for him to be friendly with the children.

Soon, my husband added his new attitude makeover to other parts of the day.

ALLOWING FAILURE

Control vs. Letting Go

My husband had to learn to "let go" of his controlling behaviors, especially with our oldest child. For example, if she wasn't studying enough. Instead of telling her that she was slacking off, I coached my husband to let her decide how much she needed to study. I told him not to make her do things that she didn't want to and to allow her to fail. All of this had to be done without disappointment or frustration in his voice and actions. He had to be more positive with his speech, exhibiting a peaceful atmosphere for his daughter. He had to realize that it was her life, not his, and it wasn't his problem.

My husband and I were both controlling individuals. My husband controlled because only perfection was good enough. If something went the slightest bit wrong he became upset, frustrated or irritated. He would become frustrated at the children for small imperfections, therefore, he did not enjoy being around the children for any length of time.

I controlled to protect my daughter from being disliked and rejected by her father, teachers and peers. To prevent rejection, I would pester my daughter to do her homework or bring a coat, etc. I constantly told her things that she could do to make her life better.

She was in sixth grade. I had to give up some control. I found out about another couple of assignments she hadn't done and considered the question, "What wouldn't I normally do...?" I wouldn't allow her to forget assignments. She'll get a poor grade.

I did just that, I let her forget.

My daughter was shocked and visibly shaken when she received her progress report a few weeks later. The assignments she missed affected her grade negatively.

I consoled her saying, "That's not your final grade for the year. You can still raise it."

She begged me not to tell Dad. She exclaimed, "He will be so disappointed in me!"

A few days later I discussed the situation with my husband. I told him, "It is vital for us to let her learn about life partially on her own. We have to let her figure out how she has the power to make things happen, not us. She has to learn for herself what she wants. In turn, you will have to act like you still love her even though she's chosen incorrectly. She must know you love her for just being her."

Having never made such a comment before, I was grateful that he respected my opinion and that he was open to the idea of allowing children to be imperfect and learn from their own mistakes. Our hope was they would strive to do their best by seeing the difference between a good effort and a minimal effort.

Days later a similar situation arose. I thought our daughter should complete a problem for school in a certain way. On this occasion I decided to tell her how I would go about working on the assignment in the form of a suggestion. My daughter disagreed with the suggestion, but later found out for herself that the suggestion had validity. Another day, a similar situation arose. I made a suggestion and she disagreed. My response was "Oh, ok. I thought you'd like this suggestion for [_____] reason, however if you think you have a better idea that is fine."

She quickly switched gears, saying she might try what had been suggested. I believed she accepted the idea because she trusted my words were just suggestions, not force. She told me later she felt guilty about always thoughtlessly dismissing my suggestions when she listened to her father's more often.

Her father soon engaged in similar behavior. Both of us internalized the slogan, "Don't worry; it's okay. This doesn't affect me."

Over time, this approach led to my oldest child becoming more conscientious in remembering tasks and responsibilities. It also helped her to remember her own physical needs, such as keeping herself warm and dry by wearing a coat.

We understood the stubbornness she displayed as a desperate want to control her own life. She reflected our pushing of forcing actions like a mirror, and similarly, our good, kind actions.

We'd changed quite a bit, actually:
• Made siblings equal
• Gave the kids our approval
• Allowed failure
• Lightened the mood by example

Let the children have some control over when and how they would handle assignments
When we let our children make some of their own decisions, they followed rules more obediently.

Here are some occasions that verified children will follow:
Our oldest daughter, I knew, was like her dad. She was a freshman in high school now and her speech was very negative. She had had an extremely hard time making friends in her private grade

school and middle school because her classmates were less than accepting. At this point, it was time for her to go to high school with the same people she'd been with for nine years now.

I saw that she was disliked and ignored all those years and it angered and frustrated me. She went to a school picnic a week prior to school opening again and the same thing happened.

She and I had a talk on the way home from the picnic about all of this and she agreed that she was rather sick of being treated unfairly. A few days before school started, we decided to send her to public school instead, so she could make friends and have a fresh start.

I knew, though, that the same problems would ensue in the public school if she weren't a more upbeat, positive person. So I asked my husband to be more positive in hope that she would copy the attitude.

My husband started using positive attitude in other parts in his life (e.g., with the kids, at work, about the weather, about traffic, etc.) and being more positive in general. The happy, unworried feeling spread and continues to grow throughout our family.[17] My daughter was able to make and keep friends much more easily and she has a group of really nice people that she hangs out with today.

Leading by Example

ACTIONS ARE IMITATED

One morning a few years ago my husband decided to cut down on fat by eliminating the margarine from his toast. My oldest saw what he had done and exclaimed "Do you expect ME to eat my toast without margarine!?" He looked surprised, without understanding her point and promptly proceeded to explain to her his intent. He ate quickly and went off to work. After her dad left, I watched how she would respond to his change. She promptly went to the toaster, toasted and prepared her toast with margarine, sat down at the table and made the statement, "I'm just not going to put jelly on my toast." It was comical but I realized that this could be a powerful tool to change her negative behaviors.

---

[17] Hebrews 10:24 We must consider how to rouse one another to love and good works.

ATTITUDE IS IMITATED

I asked my husband to try very hard to demonstrate a positive attitude in front of my daughter, especially when certain issues or problems came up. I also gave my daughter positive encouragement even for small improvements in her behavior. I asked him to say good things about other people

At one point, I noticed my oldest child and my husband again failing to pay attention to the younger children. Drawing attention to the matter, I asked my husband to make a special effort to pay close attention to the younger children and to play with them more often. My husband played with them, gave them "horseback rides," put them on his knee, and noticed the little good things about them. After only two days, my oldest child played with the younger kids. She placed them on her knee and gave them horseback rides, just like my husband. It was amazing how quickly she demonstrated the behaviors and attitudes.

In addition, my son would not play with his younger sisters. My husband, consequently, played with the two youngest daughters, setting an example for my son. Within a week he to played nicely with and accepted his younger sisters.

CHILDREN ALIGN MAINLY WITH ONE PARENT

I believed my second and fifth child exhibited my personality more than all the rest. Here are a few stories that verified my thoughts:

I had one atypical day on which I was feeling sorry for myself. I started crying. My fifth child saw me crying. The very next day, my little one, who is always happy and never cries, started crying intensely. I made sure I wouldn't feel sorry for myself again.

I had always tried to eat nutritious food, though I did not exercise regularly. Since your body is made by God, it came to my attention that I needed take care of my health better. I started doing aerobics. My second oldest daughter started doing aerobics as well. However, since I was not consistent, she soon stopped exercising altogether. Later I decided to exercise regularly and she did the same.

Again, I noticed that the oldest was like her dad.

BELIEFS ARE IMITATED

My oldest daughter, who is closer to her father, did not want to do aerobics because she thought that her father wouldn't do it. When I mentioned to her that her dad had tried aerobics, she asked me how he liked it. I told her that I thought that he liked it, and she decided, then and there, to try it sometime. Aerobics toned her, which is very important to a teenage girl, no matter how "in shape" she was from playing club basketball. The point is that my oldest daughter was not open to my ideas until my husband demonstrated openness and enthusiasm for them. She is much more willing to listen to my ideas now because my husband demonstrated that he thought my ideas had validity.

POWER AND CONTROL

Power People believe in power and control over others and their situation instead of trusting in God. Worry or fear is also involved with power. Fear disables. All people must believe that when things seem out of our control, it is God's will and He can guide us through it.

> You guide me along right paths, I fear no harm for you are at my side. Psalm 23:1-6

Another positive result of my husband's transformation was with our son's schoolwork.

In the past, my husband would be bothered by minor accidents, like someone spilling at the table or finding a missing screw. Our son reacted the same way to bad grades. If he got one wrong answer on a paper, he complained and felt badly about it. After my husband changed and did not allow little things to bother him, grades and wrong answers stopped bothering our son so much. He felt better about his accomplishments. My husband and I focused on what the kids did right in their schoolwork (e.g., how many they got right, how they knew an answer, being excited about what they knew).

After my husband noticed and focused on the positive aspect of things. He was *happier*, but he would still get frustrated when he was working with the younger kids. I knew exactly what was bothering him. I could hear it. He was using negative wording when he spoke.

The negative words made him think of all the bad things possible, and he became tense from the thoughts. I told my husband to tell the kids what he wanted them to do and focus on the good result, as opposed to what he didn't want to happen. I explained that this would result in less frustration for him and positive reaction from the kids (the kids would obey better).

It was difficult for my husband to change his speech pattern because negative words, such as don't and stop, are common in parent-speech. The words come out of our mouths almost automatically (see "Positive Speech" section). After a few months of continually trying to speak positively, my husband told me that he felt "happy and peaceful." He also mentioned that he had not gotten angry at the kids for a couple of months.

Much later, my husband confessed that he had complied with the request to say things positively, but hadn't really believed it could make any difference. However, he found that positive speech did result in a more positive reaction from the kids and better feelings for him, the parent. He is convinced that positive speech really does work. It was a surprise to him that new wording could make such a difference.

After three or four months of speaking positively, I saw the change in my husband. He was much more peaceful, which enabled him to listen to his heart and do more loving things with the children. In doing so, he was surprised at how easy it was to follow his heart and to feel good about his interactions with the children.[18]

---

[18] Matthew 11:28–30 "Come to me, all you who labor and are burdened, and I will give you rest. Take my yoke upon you and learn from me, for I am meek and humble of heart; and you will find rest for yourselves. For my yoke is easy, and my burden light."

8
LEARNING TO TRUST GOD

My husband needed to believe God would make things right when he was facing a problem. I tried to explain. He acted like he heard me but said he did not understand the point of the things I'd tell him about the Bible.

I knew he did not understand how a fall-through in plans could turn out for the good. I felt for him. He needed to let God be God instead of having a map in his mind of how things will and must go. I prayed, telling God, "It's not fair. You've got to help. Some people look at the world around them and can keep track of everything they see numbers, time, organization and concepts. Help them to understand that there are other ways that only you know the process to. You made the world, let them know you are still in charge of how the world can go."

Only a few days later I could see some breakthroughs in my husbands understanding and willingness to let go of his own scheme.

One day he brought up that he had been looking for a car to teach our oldest to drive. He said, "I tried your way of doing things. I saw the list of cars for sale and didn't want to go through searching every one of them out. I know what kind of car I'm looking for and what extras I'd like it to have for safety. I want it to be from someone who's kept up with all the oil changes and I'd like it to have a few scratches and dings on it already to keep me from getting to nervous. So, I saw the list and got this sinking feeling. It was going to be a lot of work. I let God work on it." It wasn't even a week when a woman at work mentioned her car and said she needed to sell it because her new car was soon going to come in. He knew she'd kept good maintenance on the car and it had all the criteria he was looking for. He felt so pleased.

The family is happier and peaceful now. There are still occasions when my oldest has issues because she bore the brunt of our less than perfect parenting skills early on. She is blooming now. We're so proud of all of the kids.

These stories were clinchers for understanding and believing that the things that I did changed my family and my world. I go back to God and his ways for support continually. The more I believe in God and His love, the better I can act in it and that makes all the difference.

9
KEY LEARNINGS

This section was compiled to list techniques, solutions, stories, and theories that have helped us. Several of the topics discussed earlier have been expanded upon.

Anger

Often, people subconsciously teach that they think anger is stronger than love by acting in certain ways. I was surprised when I realized that I believed in anger. Negative attitudes and anger focus on failure. Violent actions produce a variety of negative emotions and actions as well. Anger is seldom used by God; we should try to love as God loves. It is important that anger be replaced with love, especially with children because they learn everything. Using love, instead of anger, will also make you a happier person.

Love

It's important to truly believe that love is more powerful than anger. A focus on love keeps me peaceful, even when things are going wrong. When I choose to love, I choose the God of love and come closer to Him.[19] The children are much more loving and happy because they don't often see us irritated. It's so great to see smiles on

---

[19] Galatians 6:1 Brothers, even if a person is caught in some transgression, you who are spiritual should correct that one in a gentle spirit, looking to yourself, so that you also may not be tempted.

the children's faces, instead of the frowns that were there at one point. A focus on the positive resulted in the children acting with more confidence, kindness and self-esteem. Every parent and teacher hopes for these qualities in their children.

It is also very important to believe that love is what is motivating others. A person who didn't know me well surprised me with a comment when he said, "Some people don't see things like you and me." He included me as feeling and responding positively like him. I was struck by how I wanted to be the person he was assuming I was. He was right but we'd never spoken much. He was assuming that I wanted to be positive and this made me want to fulfill his expectations.

I tried this on my kids. I might say, "I bet you felt good about doing the right thing just now" in order to help my children internalize how good they felt when they exhibited positive behavior.

I might also say "you look so sweet" or "you are so nice to your sister" and they would be sweeter or nicer after I said it.

If a child was upset with another child, I helped the angry child verbalize his or her needs and concerns instead of getting angry. Teaching children how to peacefully resolve problems with others helps them learn an important skill they'll eventually need in life. If you teach your children to listen to each other, they'll get along better. When they solve disputes by themselves, it's important to praise them, so they want to repeat the same behavior.

I made a habit of being thankful to God for everything, even trials. I rejoiced instead of complaining. I did what I could and apologized when I was complacent. I decided to let God be in charge. I didn't worry about the little things, and decided that I'd do the best I could and then let God take over.

Positive Speech

Examples staying positive in speech…
Negative: Stop yelling or I'm sending you outside.
Positive: If you are quiet, you can stay inside.

Negative: Don't spill the milk!
Positive: If you pour the milk carefully the table will stay clean.

Negative: Why is your room always such a mess?
Positive: It must feel good to have a clean room.

Negative: Why don't you get your homework done on time?
Positive: I bet it feels great to be done with your homework.

Instead of using the word "no," you could fill the need by saying "You can't do this right now but you can do _____." Discuss the reason it would be a good solution and encourage the child to express his or her thoughts or emotions.

Self Esteem

A child's self-esteem is critical to his or her success in life. You can increase your children's self-esteem by teaching them new things and skills. Consider enrolling your children in classes at your local parks department or teach them yourself. The more that they learn with you participating and showing interest in their activities, the more self-confidence they will gain.

Look for the Positive

Look for the positive. You must believe that there is something positive in all situations. When my husband and I changed and began focusing on the positive, several things happened, self-esteem went up, attitude improved, and other people responded more positively to our children.

Remember to notice appropriate actions. Give examples of why something works perfectly for them. (A laminated map works well for wet and dirty hands and will last a long time. Packing a swim bag before a party will help them feel prepared and save time when time is crucial).

Positive speech is more than just the words you use. The inflections of your voice can convey acceptance or anger. Always use positive speech and, most importantly, let your children know that you love and believe in them. Love brings peace. Peace brings joy. Remember to give a little kiss on the head or a soft pat on the back when you see your child start to do what you asked.

Offer Choices; Let Go of Control

Choices are also important to children, who like to have a certain amount of control over their own lives. When my youngest two girls would not stay in bed at night, I decided to try something new. Instead of getting angry when they did not stay in bed, I decided to tell them they could keep their pillow if they stayed in bed. If they didn't, I would have the children put their pillow in the closet. (Important: I did not grab it or take it from them. If I took it from them, they would get angry.) By having them put their own pillow in the closet, they did not get angry with me. They did show disappointment, which was a chance for me to be a giver. I'd ask if they wanted to put their head on a towel (since they had put their pillow in the closet) or on one of their stuffed animals. I was still trying to help them, even after they had made the decision to give up their pillow.

When my two oldest girls went to bed late, I did not show frustration. I mentioned the positive aspects of a good night's sleep, "Enough sleep makes it easier to get up, you learn better, you are more aware, timely, and have a better attitude in the morning," I would say. These things were what they needed to focus on. I also gave them compliments if they chose an earlier bedtime, even if it was only a few minutes earlier. This helped the children acknowledge and take responsibility for their choice of bedtime.

I used positive speech and empowerment to help get my youngest two kids up in the morning. I would say, "Raise your hand if you're going to get up quickly and get ready fast!" It worked! They both raised their hands and got up. They decided they were going to get up. My youngest said she was tired and she couldn't go fast so I encouraged her by saying, "kind of fast is fine." I wanted her to feel that she would succeed. It worked.

If a child says something with anger, I ask, "How did you want to say that?" If the child says it correctly the next time, I would say something like, "I love the way you say that," or "Very nicely said." If the child doesn't want to say it correctly right away I say, "Okay, then you must say it nicely three times." If it still isn't said nicely, I say, "Okay, eight times." Once the child complies with my request, I may reduce the request based on the acceptance of the request. I feel that children deserve kindness and mercy because God is kind and merciful to all his people.

Words and Actions

When your child asks for help with something, answer "Sure" or "I'd love to help." The point here is to be cheerful and to teach them to put others first. There should be no doubt that you are glad to assist your child. Cheerfully helping your children with schoolwork teaches your child to believe that homework is okay. The tone and delivery of the words, as well as the fun you allow yourself to have with homework, will affect the way the child views schoolwork.

Patience is vital. For example, chemistry was very frustrating for my oldest child, who struggled with the homework. We knew that she wanted to be like her father, therefore I asked my husband to make a concerted effort to stay positive and patient every time he helped her with her homework. My husband made the change and now remained calm and mellow, even when my daughter became very upset and frustrated. Later, she decided to be more cheerful and accepting over things she did not understand. This was just a reflection of his acceptance of her lack of understanding. The new attitude helped her learn much more rapidly. A few months later, the oldest daughter took on the role of the patient teacher and exhibited the same calm and enduring behavior while helping one of her younger siblings during a music lesson that lasted for over an hour and a half.

Make positive comments after your children have washed their face or brushed their teeth. Positive comments will reinforce the behavior. Don't talk about how many cavities they'll have if they don't brush; rather tell them how they will protect their teeth from cavities if they brush regularly. Increase good actions by saying, "You're doing better" or "You're working harder than I've ever seen you work before!" Say things like "GRRRRREEEEAAAAT!" or use a fun or unique voice. Spell it out. Remember to smile. Notice white teeth or a clean face.

To get a child to like to take a bath, the parent can notice that the child smells good after the bath. Positive comments give approval and show loving interest in the child. Basically telling the child that he or she smells badly and needs a bath provides only negative reinforcement. It's especially important that both parents notice and appreciate good behavior, though not necessarily at the same time.

Encouraging New Behaviors

In order to get my child to want to do her hair neatly I gave a book on hair styles and bows to her. We made the hair clip together and she read and became more interested in hair styles.

To give my daughter an understanding and desire for As, I found a book on how to get As which she read and put into effect quickly. Another behavior that can significantly improve your child's interest in schoolwork is your own voiced opinions about schoolwork. Mention how much you enjoyed math, or any subject in school (even if you didn't enjoy it that much). You'll find out how much your attitude about school influences your child's interest and willingness to learn.

Instead of saying "You're not listening," say "I know I gave you a lot of instructions so let's go over them again." Your child will learn and imitate your good behaviors. If someone does something wrong it its fine to be nice and say, "Everyone makes mistakes."

People need to reevaluate why someone makes them interested or happy, basically it is so much more important to value the love and care how a person feels and sends out over any accomplishments of superficial value.

Rewards

An important part of positive reinforcement is the use of rewards. I had a habit of punishing them for bad behavior, and I gave out very few rewards for good behavior. I wanted to be much more positive and give more rewards to my children. I examined how God was with all people and I found this quote: Matthew 5:44–45, "But, I say, love your enemies! Pray for those who persecute you! In that way, you will be acting as true children of your Father in heaven. For he gives his sunlight to both the evil and the good, and he sends rain on the just and on the unjust, too." I decided to use rewards to reinforce good behavior in areas where they needed significant improvement. I did this by looking for any good behavior, even very minor actions, that I could reward. I also decided to not only use food as a reward because I was concerned about their diets. I would give them five or ten minutes later to bed, extra time playing outside, read an extra chapter in their favorite book.

Good and Kind Behavior

Practicing good and kind behavior is at the core of a happy family. It brings harmony, peace, and joy into the home. I have strived to encourage more good and kind behavior into my home as well as to weed out all negative and unkind things.

Parents should love and respect one another even if your spouse frustrates you. Realize that, with love, things will change for the better. Both parents should be responsible, hard working and trustworthy. If someone needs to change, then allow him or her to work on it.

Notice and talk about moral television programs, videos, and movies.

Parents should practice kindness often. Offer your coat to your child when he or she is cold or give the last piece of your candy as a treat. Parents should always say please and thank you to their children and to each other. Let others win games. Go that extra step to help and sacrifice. When a child hugs, hug back. Keep hugging for as long as they do, maybe longer. Pat or rub their back softly when walking past your child. Smile at them when they're working with a writing utensil. Be sympathetic to your children. Find out how they feel about things. Care about and relate to your child.

Once I asked God what I should do when my kids were bothering each other. The thought came to me to hug them. I tried it and it worked. It took away their stress, it relaxed them, and they stopped bothering each other. Discuss things lovingly and logically with your child. While helping your children, listen to their input and be interested in their reasoning. If a child is trying to talk to you, remember to acknowledge the child immediately so that when you talk to your child, he or she will mimic your responsive behavior.

Be happy when you work (no huffing, puffing, or complaining). You may say to your child, "You sure enjoy working" or "I've always liked working" or "You're doing good work." Parents need to do tasks in a timely manner so their kids will do the same.

Being logical with your kids and allow them to use logic in return. Explain your decisions. They need to hear your logic in order to be logical. Logical kids (and parents) don't get emotional about things and they tend to be easier to get along with.

Be generous to your children. Be willing to share your possessions with everyone. Sharing is easy. When you see a need, your heart will tell you what to do. Listen to the sharing idea because you want to love, not because you have to. Take the time to notice how happy it makes others feel. Support charities and let your children be involved with giving. They will imitate your generosity.

Practice helping your children and they will copy your actions and become more helpful to other children, and even other adults. If you are willing to take the time to help out, your kids will also take the time to help.

Look lovingly at your kids, even when they do something incorrectly or wrong. This will teach your children to be kind to others when they are wronged. Your kids will learn to forgive and love their siblings and friends.

Be patient. If a child demonstrates that they need more patience, have the child practice patience five times, waiting one minute in between. While the child is practicing patience, remember to notice something the child did correctly and comment on this. Remember, when you are correcting your child's behavior, you need to be eternally patient, kind, and loving. There can be no anger, malice, or frustration. Later, reinforce that you see them being patient in some aspect of their life.

You must become what you want them to be. You need to look at yourself and evaluate how and where you need to change. You can change. Do these things because you love them and you want them to have good behaviors. If you force them to do something, they will become stubborn and resist. They want to be like you, so their response of "no," is a reflection of your pushy stubbornness.

Be gentle. Touch softly. Children remember and copy touch as well as language.

If a child will not hold your hand, put your finger in the child's hand and see if he or she will hold it. If the child won't do it, do it slowly and gently again. Eventually, the child will take it. Always be gentle and calm. During my first years as a parent, I believed kids would not listen. When I exhibited this belief, by getting angry and frustrated, my children believed me and became what I expected them to be. When I started believing they would be good, had good intentions, and wanted to understand, they responded positively.

Another idea I had was to put up a dry erase board or a bulletin board in a place they passed by often and could see it. I wrote little love notes and encouraging messages on the board for them to see. Show your children's good schoolwork to others and tell them how proud you are of them. Tape it up on the mirror, refrigerator, or wall.

Allow your children to groom you (e.g., comb your hair, apply nail polish). Your trust in them helps them trust you more.

If your child does not want to share, offer the child something of yours. Offer with only kind sounds in your voice (Remember: no anger or resentment to the child who would not share.). If you act kindly but sound angry, your children will remember your anger and forget the act.

You must be drawn to kindness in voice, words and action. It's important for parents to constantly critique themselves and change their bad qualities. Clean up what you have running through your mind. You must get rid of all profanity (this includes saying, "Oh my God!"). Try to whisper, instead of shouting.

Allow your children to help choose what they will wear. Tell them if they wear *this*, they will be warm. If you wear *this*, they will be cool for the hot day. If the child decides differently than you would, you can say, "Okay, if you get too hot, you can roll up your sleeves," or something like that. Help them find an answer. Ultimately this will help the children trust your judgment because you have allowed them to make a decision.

Wanting to obey God allowed me to change the way I dealt with people and situations. God's word taught me that people are not evil, only mistaken. This notion enabled me to have more love for all others. If you keep trying to do the right thing, eventually the positive, good behavior will spread. Say, "I love you," especially when there has been trouble. Say, "I love you," often. Say, "I love you," to your spouse. Say it to each of your children.

Demonstrate kind behavior in all aspects of life. Husbands should happily help their wives in all tasks. It's also important that they look for what needs to be done instead of waiting for their wife to ask for help. When husbands cheerfully help their wives, they're demonstrating their love for them. The wife should not be a slave to the family. Husbands and wives should show willing and loving support for each other and for the family. *They are a team.* You and your spouse's willingness to help one another will be seen and imitated by your children. *Strive to be kind and get along with your spouse at all times: avoid anger and frustration, give positive reinforcement to each other, tell your kids how well your spouse is doing, and let them know that you are willing to try each other's ideas.* This is so important!

Happiness in the Home

For the longest time, our children rarely laughed or smiled. Small mistakes made them feel nervous and unloved. Observing this, I asked my husband to be more cheerful and calm when little things went wrong. I also asked him to laugh when the kids tried to make a joke and to start being more joyful. He resisted a little at first, but he tried to do what I had asked and our home became more relaxed. All the kids became happier. I also asked my husband to try not to dwell on report card grades that were less than an A, but rather to praise them for all their good work. My husband started to joke and good-naturedly tease the kids a little, making them even happier. As a result of my husband's changes, all of the children started to exhibit more joy and love between each other and with their friends.

Re-evaluate Your Priorities and Listening to Your Heart

Be ready to follow Christ and do His will. When a problem comes up, ask God what you should do and listen to His answer. God will answer you with the first good thought that you have.

Are problems really that bad? Do you need to get upset when things don't go exactly as you have planned? Teach your children how to deal with problems in a positive way. Listen to your heart and follow that idea. When you use an idea from your heart and it works, remember to thank God and remember to mention to your children how God is helping you.

Remember: Follow the first good thought that comes to your heart.[20][21]

---

[20] Galatians 4:6–7 As proof that you are children, God sent the spirit of his son into our hearts, crying out, "Abba, Father!" So you are no longer a slave but a child, and if a child then also an heir, through God.

[21] Proverbs 3:5–6 Trust in the Lord with all your heart, on your own intelligence rely not; In all your ways be mindful of him, and he will make straight your paths.

It's important to actively look for opportunities to practice goodness and kindness during the day and to discuss these opportunities with your children. Let them know that you are trying to be good and kind, just like Christ. They will try to be like Christ, in time, also.

Loving God

Be amazed at the things God has worked out. Remember Abraham and Sarah in Genesis 12 and how they left everything they had to do God's will? They searched for a city built by God somewhere in the desert. That sounds realistic, doesn't it? They didn't know where they were going, but they went unquestioningly because they had faith in God's plan.[22]

Being born again means having a new life in God by doing God's will. You can do God's will by listening to Him in your heart and applying his ways to your actions, attitude, thoughts, and speech. Following God's will often means acting on the spontaneous, kind thoughts you have that you normally wouldn't act upon.

If a person makes a mistake, a helpful comment might be, "Everyone makes mistakes." An adult can also demonstrate forgiveness by saying this when another driver makes a mistake. Spread forgiveness and practice forgiving everyone, all the time. *Witness the goodness of God to the ends of the earth.*

Do more than is expected of you in order to show God how much you love Him. Give generously to God. Let everything be up to Him.[23]

Everyone needs to realize that God is the driver and they are the passenger in the automobile of life. Don't try to be too controlling. Accept life's detours and setbacks with humility and patience. Be assured that there is a reason for everything and that God has only the best in mind for you.

---

[22] Colossians 1:9 Therefore, from the day we heard this, we do not cease praying for you and asking that you may be filled with the knowledge of his will through all spiritual wisdom and understanding

[23] James 1:27 Religion that is pure and undefiled before God and the Father is this: to care for orphans and widows in their affliction and to keep oneself unstained by the world.

Family Peace is Found by Using God's Ways

Remember: God loves a cheerful giver. Never question God's paths when it looks as though things are going badly. Trust Him always.

God, who is true, promises to save us if we turn from all our wicked ways. His promise REQUIRES us to find where we have turned away from Him and His ways. If we have blamed others, we must turn toward goodness, patience, acceptance, love and forgiveness in thought and ACTION. That is who God is. We MUST be truthful and honest. We MUST do our very best to make up for past grievances.

Change the World by Loving God and Your Neighbor

Anytime you interact with a person, you should say your words with love. God is love. Do everything with a Godly mindset.

Does anyone really think the world can be changed? If they do, they must focus on changing themselves. Who thinks that backbiting, anger, or acquiring more material possessions will fix the world? We must start with changing who we are. Ask God to show you your faults. Many years ago, I didn't think I had much left to change because I followed all the laws and rules. I'm still finding and working on fixing my faults. Trying to suppress bad behavior doesn't work nearly as well as following your heart. When you follow your heart, your mind turns toward God and it's easier to be "good" because you think instead about what you should be doing rather than all the things you can't do. The world around you will start falling into place.

Happiness is found when you realize that God is glad to help even though we still have many predicaments to deal with. We must keep trying and pray that God continues to help us; He will if we are willing to change ourselves.

If you have a false god, will you go to heaven? Do you have to love God and all others to go to heaven? Jesus gave two new commandments: to love God and to love your neighbor. He said, "If you follow these commandments, the other commandments will come naturally."

Let nothing own you. Keep Sunday for God (keep holy the Sabbath). If you do something or think about something often, try to take it off your mental to-do list on Sunday. Relax, love, and pray.

Here's an excellent Bible passage that helps explain the rules for a new life: Notice who is an idol worshiper in the last sentence of this passage.

Ephesians 4:25–5:5 Therefore, putting away falsehood, speak the truth, each one to his neighbor, for we are members one of another. Be angry but do not sin; do not let the sun set on your anger, and do not leave room for the devil. The thief must no longer steal, but rather labor, doing honest work with his [own] hands, so that he may have something to share with one in need. No foul language should come out of your mouths, but only such as is good for needed edification, that it may impart grace to those who hear. And do not grieve the Holy Spirit of God, with which you were sealed for the day of redemption. All bitterness, fury, anger, shouting, and reviling must be removed from you along with all malice. [And] be kind to one another, compassionate, forgiving one another as God has forgiven you in Christ. So be imitators of God, as beloved children, and live in love, as Christ loved us and handed himself over for us as a sacrificial offering to God for a fragrant aroma. Immorality or any impurity or greed must not even be mentioned among you, as is fitting among holy ones, no obscenity or silly or suggestive talk, which is out of place, but instead, thanksgiving. Be sure of this, that no immoral or impure or greedy person, that is, an idolater, has any inheritance in the kingdom of Christ and of God.

Who is Your God?

Let's go back to square one: Who is God? What is He in control of? Where is He? Does He care? Does He know? Does He love? Does He forgive? Is He harsh with you every time you falter? Does He lovingly call you back and let you keep trying? Is He there for you? Is He honest? Is He faithful? Is He just? Does He care for everyone or just the people around him who talk to Him? Does He seek to help the hurting, helpless, unintelligent, poor, sick, dying, and those who are alone? Because people are like their god, you can reassess your life by checking who you are against Him. This will lead you to see if you have any false gods in your life. Once you find your false gods, do everything to eradicate them from your life.

False gods are what make you fall hardest. Remember, God has power and you must have faith and will. If it makes you angry when someone changes your plans or gets in your way, you must let go of that too. Confess all to the real God. Repent and ask to see if you still have false gods.

Keep Trying

If your problems seem as though they're staying, you must have faith and keep trying. You might get discouraged, but do not go back to the old ways. For courage and hope, try again. You'll succeed more and more often. You will get it right eventually and positive actions will become second nature to you. Keep trying! Keep track of your successes either in your mind or write them down. Think of your past successes instead of being discouraged because you're not where you want to be. Believe that you want the happiness that is only found by doing God's will.

If you're having trouble changing a particular behavior or attitude, pretend that you are another person (like acting) whom you have seen exhibit the desired behavior or attitude. This has helped me with difficult changes.

10
EVALUATION

I evaluated my family and myself by using the beliefs listed below.

Acknowledgment

- In order to change, admit that you know very little.[24][25]
- Just as parents will take care of their children, believe God will take care of you. He has your best interests in mind.
- Have hope and forget your fears. (Hope gives a path. Fear disables.)
- Believe only in the true God of love.
- Know who God is. He is full love, kindness, and is slow to anger.
- Acknowledge all that God has done in history starting with making the entire world.

---

[24] John 17:22–23 And I have given them the glory you gave me, so that they may be one as we are one: I in them and you in me that they may be brought to perfection as one, that the world may know that you sent me, and that you loved them even as you loved me.

[25] James 1:5 But if any of you lacks wisdom, he should ask God, who gives to all generously and ungrudgingly, and he will be given it.

- Know what God expects of his people, like children need to do what their parents expect of them. These are things that will help build character. Obey God's laws, love God, and care about your neighbor. Since He is the author of love, do what he would do.
- Be peaceful. God does not expect excitement all the time.
- Assess who or what other gods you have. What is on your mind most often? (The true God of love should be in your mind and heart always.) Put all things but true needs out of your mind. Reassess everything you — Are you doing what God is directing you to do?
- Simplify life. Get rid of things. Free up time. Value family and people over things and wants
- Check your responses and actions — are you doing all things in a loving way?
- Clean up your mouth. Profanity should not exist in the home. Leave God's name for talking about or to God only. Discard rough or profane words from your vocabulary. Do not say, "Oh my God!" or "Oh my Lord!" These are inappropriate uses of God's name. There are both blessings and curses for the use of the Lord's name[26]. Exodus 20:7 tells us, "You shall not take the name of the LORD your God in vain, for the LORD will not leave him unpunished who takes His name in vain."
- Try being calm or quieter instead of verbalizing so much excitement.
- Do you get along with everyone, especially your spouse? Do you criticize or bring up negative things about your spouse or others? Do not demean your spouse by referring to him or her as a "child." Do you tease your spouse or kids in a mean-spirited way? Your children, in some way, will mimic these behaviors. You can love and change your children's and grandchildren's future.
- Accept and respect others' likes and dislikes for trivial things. You don't have to convince someone to think your way (i.e., colors, tastes, preferences).

---

[26] John 15:16 You did not choose me, but I chose you and appointed you to go and bear fruit—fruit that will last. Then the Father will give you whatever you ask in my name.

- Acknowledge that you don't know how to do some things correctly. Say you are sorry to God.[27] God commands us to repent to Him of our ignorance as to what we worship.[28]
- Acknowledge your faults and failings and ask God to forgive you too. After you have confessed your sins, focus on what you will do next. No one is perfect. The way you learned to parent may not be the best way. The way you respond to trials can be changed. Try God's ever-loving, kind, and gentle ways. Desire to learn how to be a better parent. Be willing to experiment and try new parenting techniques. Desire to do the right thing for God, using His loving ways. He is your goal and should be on your mind constantly.
- Remember all people are your brothers and sisters. God's biggest commandment, after loving Him, is to love your neighbor as yourself.
- Apologize and actively make amends for past grievances.
- Romans 12:2. Do not conform yourself to this age. But be transformed by the renewal of your mind, that you may discern what is the will of God, what is good and pleasing and perfect.
- Be thankful, not picky. If you're picky, your kids will be also.

Believe

- Believe all of God's words.[29][30][31] Remember that children are a gift to you from God.

---

[27] Acts 17:29,30 "Since therefore we are the offspring of God, we ought not to think that the divinity is like an image fashioned from gold, silver, or stone by human art and imagination. God has overlooked the times of ignorance, but now he demands that all people everywhere repent because he has established a day on which he will 'judge the world with justice' through a man he has appointed, and he has provided confirmation for all by raising him from the dead."

[28] 1 John 2:15–17 Do not love the world or anything in the world. If anyone loves the world, the love of the Father is not in him. For everything in the world—the cravings of sinful man, the lust of his eyes and the boasting of what he has and does—comes not from the Father but from the world. The world and its desires pass away, but the man who does the will of God lives forever.

[29] 1 John 1:8–9 If we say, "We are without sin," we deceive ourselves, and the truth is not in us. If we acknowledge our sins, he is faithful and just and will forgive our sins and cleanse us from every wrongdoing.

[30] John 8:31–32 Jesus then said to those Jews who believed in him, "If you remain in my word, you will truly be my disciples, and you will know the truth, and the truth will set you free."

- Believe in Jesus' command of love.[32 33 34 35 36]
- Believe that God loves you and cares about you.
- Believe that He will help you if you ask Him and seek Him.

Take Action

- Fast or do penance.[37 38 39 40]
- Pray together. Ask for the loving hopes of your heart. Ask for help to continue to find God's ways and improve. Pray about it every day. Ask God to make you more peaceful and loving. When you act in peace and love, you calm down.
- Ask God to make you more like Jesus. Accept the fact that you need to change.

---

[31] John 11:25–26 Jesus said to her, "I am the resurrection and the life; whoever believes in me, even if he dies, will live, and everyone who lives and believes in me will never die. Do you believe this? "

[32] Philippians 2:3-4 Do nothing out of selfish ambition or vain conceit, but in humility consider others better than yourselves. Each of you should look not only to your own interests, but also to the interests of others.

[33] Rom. 12:9,19–21 Let love be sincere; hate what is evil, hold on to what is good; 19 Beloved, do not look for revenge but leave room for the wrath; for it is written, "Vengeance is mine, I will repay, says the Lord." Rather, "if your enemy is hungry, feed him, if he is thirsty, give him to drink; for by doing so you will heap burning coals on his head." Do not be conquered by evil but conquer evil with good. (i.e. good actions, attitudes, and words)

[34] John 15:12–13 This is my commandment; love one another as I love you. No one has greater love than this, to lay down one's life for one's friends.

[35] Romans 15:1–2,4 We who are strong ought to put up with the failings of the weak and not to please ourselves; let each of us please our neighbor for the good, for building up. 4 For whatever was written for our instruction, that by endurance and by the encouragement of the scriptures we might have hope.

[36] John 13:34–35 I give you a new commandment: love one another. As I have loved you, so you also should love one another. This is how all will know that you are my disciples, if you have love for one another.

[37] Joel 1:14 Proclaim a fast, call an assembly; Gather the elders, all who dwell in the land, into the house of the Lord, your God, and cry to the Lord, your God, and cry to the Lord!

[38] Proverbs 15:33 The fear of the Lord is training for wisdom, and humility goes before honors.

[39] Judges 20 The Lord does not want holocausts and peace offering but a contrite heart with weeping and fasting.

[40] Psalm 34:17–18 The righteous cry out, and the Lord hears them; he delivers them from all their troubles. The Lord is close to the brokenhearted and saves those who are crushed in Spirit.

- Examine your conscience. Do you speak kindly and quietly without looking or acting angry? Allow your voice to sound peaceful. Choose words and actions that have kind and peaceful connotations. You do choose! If you don't know how to "put on peace," observe other peaceful people and imitate them. From love comes peace; from peace comes joy. Everyone is capable of finding joy. At one point, God told me that joy was coming. I decided that I needed to keep believing that joy was coming because the words were not from me.

- While you are still transitioning from your old ways to becoming more positive, you need to be quiet and gather your thoughts before speaking.

- It is important to speak with love and kindness to older children as well as younger ones. If a parent speaks with love to a three-year-old child, the parent should speak with love to a teenager as well, even when correcting the teenager. Keep believing in love. Know that the love the child experiences will eventually be given back to you by the child.[41][42][43]

- Dispose of all preconceived notions about your child and other people. Expect the best. Don't hold on to past problems. Forgive and forget. Dwell on how God loves you. Enjoy the world that God has created for you (e.g., see how God loves you in the beautiful trees and mountains around us). Think and believe. Just as nature is always around us, so God shows He is with us at all times and we should not worry.

- Kids will reflect what they experience in their environment (parents, teachers, TV, videos, books, music, etc.). Keep this in mind. Remove what you feel are not God's ways (unkind actions, naughtiness, rudeness, profanity, loudness, etc.). Start by cleaning one room and work your way through your home.

---

[41] James 3:17 But the wisdom that comes from heaven is first of all pure; then peace-loving, considerate, submissive, full of mercy and good fruit, impartial and sincere.

[42] Hebrews 12:15 See to it that no one misses the grace of God and that no bitter root grows up to cause trouble and defile many.

[43] Ephesians 4:32 Be kind and compassionate to one another, forgiving each other, just as in Christ God forgave you.

- Lead by example. Your children will be a reflection of you (whether good or bad). If you expect your children to be calm, you must be calm also, even when things go wrong. If you expect your children to love, you must also act lovingly.
  - A soft touch
  - A soft word
  - A smile
  - The words "I care" and "I love you"
- If you have too much to do, do what you can and don't worry about it. You'll get to it when you get to it.
- Be thankful and express it always — to God and others.
- Treat your children with absolute acceptance if they fail.
- Mention what you like about their actions, reactions, and work. Always use positive speech. Do this daily. Remind yourself to continue to stay positive and look for the good in all things and people. Keep these things in your mind; it must become natural for you to be this way. Spouses should check and remind one another (again, with love) how and what they say.[44]
- When something bothers you about your child or others, focus on the smallest good things — in the child, in the people around you, or your job. If it is difficult for you to see any happiness or good in the world around you, focus on the smallest good you can. The negative perspective needs to be erased.
- Be hopeful; express it.
- Tell your children, "I like what you look like: your nice hands, your nice hair, your nose, voice."
- Apologize to your children when you make mistakes. This will teach them that you are human, capable of mistakes, and need forgiveness. It will also teach your children to forgive.
- Work to make things easier and more efficient. Organize. *Keep only what you need.* Make frequent trips to St. Vincent de Paul or to your local donation center.

---

[44] Proverbs 3:3–4 Let love and faithfulness never leave you: bind them around your neck, write them on the tablet of your heart. Then you will win favor and good name in the sight of God and man.

- Focus on logic. If something falls, pick it up. If you spill, clean it up.
- If a need arises, stop what you're doing and do what you can to help. Prioritize others' needs above your own. Stop and smell the flowers with your kids. Life's too short to miss the wondrous things that your children are experiencing. Share it with them with wonder and delight. These are the things that you, and your children, will remember forever.
- Offer help when possible. Again, your children will see this and imitate it.
- Focus on what you want to happen in all situations. If you want a baby to stop crying, you should think about how to make him or her happy. Ask yourself, "How can I?" You'll have an idea in your heart that is good, then do it. We want to believe in hope, not fear.
- Decide to treat people always with love:
    - Strangers
    - While you're driving
    - In the store
    - On the telephone
    - In the workplace
    - Your spouse
    - Your children

Expect

- Ask God for new ways to be kind and generous. When you think of them, follow through with it. It is a gift, not payment for future leverage. Do it because of love. Do it even if you will have almost nothing left. It is okay to give all you have of something considering these material things were given to you. If you are meant to have them again, then they will come back to you somehow. Call on the name of the Lord and listen for what He says because The Word is near you, in your mouth and in your heart.[45][46]

---

[45] Jeremiah 29:11 "for I know the plans I have for you," declares the Lord, "plans to prosper you and not to harm you, plans to give you hope and a future."

[46] Proverbs 4:20–22 My son, pay attention to what I say; listen closely to my words. Do not let them out of your sight, keep them within your heart; for they are life to those who find them and health to a man's whole body.

- One day I was dwelling on the idea of having faith in God and expecting whatever He says to do will eventfully unravel the big mess I'd slowly been undoing in my family. At that same time my child brought me a black string she wanted untangled. I sat down in the family room. The shades were down and the lights were off in the room. Some light was coming into the family room from cracks in the shades and light from another room. I could see the string in my hand but could not distinguish one loop from the next because of the darkness. As I sat there the thought came to me "just pull right there." I pinched at the mass of string and pulled. The knot began to give way. I pulled more and with satisfaction saw the knot was coming undone. A few more pulls and the knot disappeared. I was in awe. I thought, *that's exactly how we get out tough situations.* We have to believe there's going to be a way out and we have to listen and do what we're told.
- Expect things to go well. If you don't know how to get the behavior you want, accept that now is not the time. Don't try too hard to get it. Wait. If you wait, it will happen if and when it is supposed to happen.

Listen to Your Heart

Listen to the first thought that comes to you even if you don't have a solution. Expect and listen for an answer from your heart. The solution may be very different than you would expect but you need to listen to your heart. Make sure to follow through with your thought. God will show you the way. It's not that we need to keep praying for what we need fixed, but rather pray and believe that if we have asked, and it is God's will, He will lead us out of the problem. Follow or do what God is asking you to do right now. Put the problem into His hands and do what your heart tells you. This is a difficult thing to do sometimes because our heart may surprise us with something unexpected.[47][48][49][50][51][52] When I waited for something, I would suddenly get an idea that was surprising and unexpected, as though I would never be creative or clever enough to think of

---

[47] Romans 10:6,8 But the righteousness that comes from faith says…"The word is near you, in your mouth and in your heart."

something like *that*. I would get the idea right when I'd finally let go and said, "Okay fine, God, you take care of it because I can't think of anything." This new approach was easy. I did not stress about details. Usually the details fell into place easily. If, on occasion, the ideas fell through, I'd let them go. Acceptance of every road he sent me on was important to keep me selfless. The words "being self-less" sound terrible. These words sounded to me like nothing good would come to you or you'll do nothing. I'd have to say that's incorrect. God has many good experiences in store for everyone.

Accept the Answer

- Stay calm while working through problems. Logically fix the problem without getting upset. Remember that things happen for a reason and you can take these opportunities to teach yourself and others. Continue to believe in gentle actions and reactions. Focus lovingly on what you can do to fix the problem and also on how you can help.
- When things work out well, thank God. When things don't work, believe there is a reason and thank God.
- Have no preconceived ideas of how something must go — accept how things unfold, even if they don't happen exactly as you've planned. Things happen for a reason; be open about it.

---

[48] Romans 12:1–2 Therefore, I urge you, brothers, in view of God's mercy, to offer your bodies as living sacrifices, holy and pleasing to God—this is your spiritual act of worship. Do not conform any longer to the pattern of this world, but be transformed by the renewing of your mind. Then you will be able to test and approve what God's will is—his good, pleasing and perfect will

[49] Galatians 5:1 It is for freedom that Christ has set us free. Stand firm then, and do not let yourselves be burdened again by a yoke of slavery.

[50] Lamentations 3:22–24 Because of the Lord's great love we are not consumed, for his compassions never fail. They are new every morning; great is your faithfulness. I say to myself, "The Lord is my portion; therefore I will wait for him."

[51] Revelation 7:17 For the Lamb at the center of the throne will be their shepherd; he will lead them to springs of living water. And God will wipe away every tear from their eyes.

[52] Romans 10:9–14 For if you confess with your mouth that Jesus is Lord and believe in your heart that God raised him from the dead you will be saved...the same Lord is Lord of all, enriching all who call upon him. For everyone who calls on the name of the Lord will be saved. But how can they call on him in whom they have not believed?

Obey

- Remember to do your daily work.
- Do your work cheerfully, and your children will also.
- Do what you wouldn't normally do.

Continue To Love and Encourage

- Keep showing mercy, love, and positive encouragement.
- Visualize doing and saying good things for upcoming opportunities and in times of trial.
- Find opportunities to praise your kids. Praise them when they are being Christian and showing goodness, kindness, patience, and understanding. Praise will promote more of this behavior.
- Take photos of the kids and post them when they are being good and loving in order to promote those behaviors
- Love your children's beautiful little hands; count their toes; look into their eyes. Comment on and find something to love about their looks. Tell them how much you love them.
- Talk about the day they were born and how good you felt when they came into the world. Talk about how excited everyone was about their arrival. Do not talk about negative things. It is important for children to know they are wanted and loved, not a burden on their parents.
- Tell them "I love you," especially when things go wrong. Say it to them joyfully. Practice unconditional love.
- Put up school papers on your family bulletin board or refrigerator. Find something good in them, especially if you want to promote a certain behavior or skill.
- Notice them saying something nice and praise them.
- Don't talk to others about your kid's faults or past faults. Talking about it will encourage more of the same. Instead, talk about the things that they are doing well or how much they are trying to be good at something. Avoid talking about the bad things you know about. Talk about the good things that have happened or are happening.
- Ask children questions with expectations. For example, "How are you doing on your homework?" "Who wants to do _____?" "How much did you do?" The point is instead of

making them act a certain way, getting them to think about how they are doing it. Even when the kids are supposed to be working on their homework, ask them how far they've gotten on it, or if they need any assistance instead of asking, "Are you doing your homework?" This shows that you expect good out of them.

- Look for the good and the rainbows (joy) will spread.
- In order to teach polite speech, we must let children fulfill themselves — not the parents. Believe that they are doing their best and watch them go, do not force them to do anything. If you are less controlling, your children will listen and obey you more willingly because they know that you trust them.
- Teach them to communicate before they can talk. When they want food, say, "May I have a bottle?" If they make a noise, tell them, "Good, you said 'May I have _____.'" Then you say, "Yes, you may have a _____." The point is to teach them how to ask and answer politely at an early age. This will make it easier later.
- Be glad to serve. Smile and answer with a happy, "Sure I will!" Your children will reflect your demonstration of happiness.
- When children give something to someone, tell them how good that must make them feel and how happy the other person feels. Praise them for loving others.
- When we believe in the good (good comes from loving others and doing what we are called to do) we are released from being bound by our passions and desires. Love conquers all.

Galatians 4:31: Therefore, brothers, we are children not of the slave woman but of the freeborn woman

This verse talks about Sarah, who follows God, is not a slave, but free. She is not bound to evil because God decides where to lead her and He is her guide.

- When one child is hurt by another, try hugging both, accepting both, and talking to both with kindness and understanding. Speak with love and logic, not emotion.

• Give the glory to God. When things are going well, tell your child how much God is helping you. When things are not going well, be cheerful and say, "There must be a reason."

We have decided that anything that spreads goodness can stay in our family and, with no exception, all else must be thrown away.

II

CONCLUSION

On the road of life, simply following the commandments is not enough. I found out later that I had to do more than just "know" the commandments and stay out of trouble. Rather, I realized I needed to look for ways to actively fulfill God's will by loving others with my words, actions, and deeds. My work started within my family, but now I want to spread love by helping others when God allows me to know their troubles. I realize now that everyone is part of my family.[53]

People who react with love are usually happy, peaceful, confident, and patient because they are people who believe in love. I felt all these things when I acted in this manner. Our children, though it may have taken a while, believed in these new ways and copied them. I continued to focus on being a problem-fixer with the hope that my kids would become people who look for and find solutions that God will accept.

Parents should realize that their fears are transferred to their children, at least to an extent. When parents have act stressed, their child, consequently, will copy their behavior. Common results are either nervous or emotional reactions from the child; both may be

---

[53] Galatians 3:26–28 You are all sons of God through faith in Christ Jesus, for all of you who were baptized into Christ have clothed yourselves with Christ. There is neither Jew nor Greek, slave nor free, male nor female, for you are all one in Christ Jesus.

difficult to deal with. If you can identify and eliminate fear, your kids will be less nervous and emotional. Children who are less nervous and emotional are easier to manage, which results in overall harmony for the family.

Harmony results from love, peace, and hope (an absence of fears). Children do copy uncaring inaction, actions, emotions, and reactions. Decide to look for where you need to make changes in your actions to help others.

Seeing your kindness spread into your children's lives is truly the most rewarding part of the whole process.[54][55]

---

[54]1 Peter 1:8–9 Though you have not seen him, you love him; and even though you do not see him now, you believe in him and are filled with an inexpressible and glorious joy, for you are receiving the goal of your faith, the salvation of your souls.

[55]1 Peter 5:6–7 Humble yourselves, therefore, under God's mighty hand, that he may lift you up in due time. Cast all your anxiety on him, because he cares for you.